The
OTHER SIDE
of the Storm

Recovering From Your Husband's
Porn Addiction

Brittany Richardson
(with Joshua Richardson)

COBB PUBLISHING
2019

Published in the United States of America by:

Cobb Publishing
704 E. Main St.
Charleston, AR 72933
CobbPublishing.com
CobbPublishing@gmail.com

ISBN: 978-1-947622-38-8

CONTENTS

To those who help us fight for our marriage.

Thank You.

This book is dedicated to you.

INTRODUCTION

It's 5:48 a.m. Joshua left for work almost two hours ago. It's dark and stormy and I can't sleep. I miss the warmth of my husband beside me in bed. I miss the tender kisses he bestows on me as he prepares to leave. I yearn to be with him. I know the next ten hours will crawl by until I'm in his arms again.

The newborn gets fussy and I crawl out of bed. Wandering through the kitchen, I try to decide if I should abandon the idea of sleep and just face the day.

I notice something white taped to the coffee pot.

It's a note from him.

"Press power button for two cups of decaf Joe!" – S.S.C.

I smile. I love that man. In the wee hours of the morning, he thought of me and how he could brighten my day. He remembers the little details about me, like how I love coffee but can't drink the "real" stuff. He adds his initials from my pet name for him and proves again that he's my "Sweet Southern Charmer."

All mine.

No marriage is perfect. We don't live in a fairytale. And yet sometimes I think we get pretty close. This is my everyday life with a man who sacrifices his all for me and who constantly thinks of ways to demonstrate his love. I trust my whole heart to him. Together, we are strong. Together, we overcome.

This is our life after porn.

Looking back over the days following the initial blow that pornography dealt our marriage, I see how much has changed for the better. I wish I could have seen then what we have now. I want to go back and tell myself, "Hold on. It's gonna be okay. This is going to be beautiful."

I can't reach back to that hopeless young woman, desperately searching for a way out. I can't comfort her and tell her that things will get better.

But I can tell you.

Right now, maybe you're steeped in a depression so dark, you wonder if you will ever feel again. Maybe you question everything about yourself, your spouse, and everyone around you. You trust no one, and you're sure you never will again. You're broken. Beaten.

Hold on.

This is not over. God is not done.

Our Heavenly Father makes all things new. He creates beauty in the chaos. He picks up the broken pieces that fall from those pedestals and refashions them into something more wondrous. Something more authentic. Something real.

The days will be dark. The nights will seem endless. You will feel like you're wading through quicksand. Every step will be shaky. Every moment will have pain.

But hold on. Don't let go. It won't always be this way. You are in the middle of a storm. But storms always—*always*—come to an end.

It's gonna be okay.

Maybe not today. Maybe not tomorrow. But it will be okay. He promised.

> *And we know that all things work together*
> *for good to them that love God, to them*
> *who are the called according to His pur-*
> *pose (Romans 8:28).*

Do you love the Lord? Are you His, first and foremost? Then it's going to be okay.

I can't tell you everything will work out the way you want. I can't even promise that your marriage will recover. That takes two people with hearts committed—to God first and each other second. I can't force that on either you or your husband.

What I can promise you is that, no matter what, Christ is still King. He is still the Great Physician. He binds and heals wounds. He can rescue and restore even the most shattered relationships. He is able.

Your marriage is no exception.

This is going to be beautiful.

Five years ago I thought our marriage was over. I thought that any happiness we once had was permanently blotted out. I was scared, and I felt alone. Even now, remembering the pain from the revelation of my husband's betrayal can bring tears to my eyes. I can still remember the nausea that washed over me as it dawned on me that lies had been woven throughout our entire marriage.

It was ugly. Twisted. Satan was rejoicing. And yet, as always, God was at work. He took the frayed edges, the unraveling threads, the stained fabric of our past, and He wove a new pattern.

We started again. Not removed from the consequences of sin. But stronger for the struggle.

I wouldn't trade my marriage for any other marriage in the world. I wouldn't even go back to that blissful honeymoon period when I thought our marriage really was perfect. What we have now is deeper, more enduring. It is worth the fight.

If you're in that place of brokenness, where hope is elusive and shadows engulf, just wait. One more day. One more hour.

This can be beautiful.

The storm is over. The sun is rising. A light mist makes the grass sparkle, and the birds are chirping once more.

I love the beauty that follows a storm.

CHAPTER 1:
CONFESSIONS OF A FORMER PORN ADDICT'S WIFE

I had never cried so hard, nor felt so broken. A rage boiled through my veins fiercer than I'd ever experienced. The intensity of my fury frightened me. The weight of hopelessness and desperation crushed me until I felt physically beaten. I wanted to scream. I wanted to vomit. I wanted to break something. Or someone.

It was a Monday evening, overcast and grey. An unusually cool Arkansas breeze blew against the window as I scurried about the house. Supper would be late. It had already been a day full of disappointments and I struggled against tears the whole day. I took a break from my work, and was startled out of my thoughts by a knock on the front door. Joshua, home from work two hours early! I was so glad to see him, so thankful he had gotten off early and could help me with the children, who seemed particularly determined to drive me insane.

Joshua stepped inside and took me in his arms. I immediately sensed that something was wrong. He whispered gravely, "We need to talk." Taking my hand, he pulled me toward the couch. The worst possible scenarios flashed through my mind and I braced myself as I sat down beside him. My heart pounded. My hands trembled. My head spun. His voice was thick when he finally spoke. "I've lied to you."

A few days prior to this, a fussy baby kept me up in the middle of the night. I picked up Joshua's phone, intending to surf the web while trying to rock our second-born back to sleep. The internet browser was already open. It was set to search images.

I didn't want to jump to any conclusions. I investigated a little further, but couldn't find anything suspicious in the search history. Deciding there was probably nothing inappropriate about whatever Joshua had been searching online, I eventually tucked the sleeping baby back in his crib and crawled into bed. Joshua rolled over and wrapped his arm around me. I was reasonably certain there was nothing to my fleeting suspicions, but I felt compelled to make sure.

"When was the last time you looked at porn?"

"What?"

Somewhat impatiently, I asked again, "When was the last time you looked at pornography?"

"I don't know." There was a long silence. "Sometime back before we were married."

I knew Joshua had struggled with pornography before we got married. He told me this before we ever began courting and had asked my forgiveness. Now, lying beside my husband in the darkness, I had to make a choice: trust that he was telling me the truth and had remained faithful since our wedding, or go crazy questioning every move he would make in the weeks to come. Doubt and suspicion are vile companions. I had lived with them before, and the past had proved them needless weights in our marriage. So, I chose to trust.

But sitting there several days later, Joshua in tears confessed that he had lied—he had been using pornography off and on for the last year. I listened quietly and watched as my strong husband fell to pieces before me. I had never seen Joshua cry before. Now he sobbed, begged my forgiveness, and swore he would never do it again.

If you have ever experienced a similar betrayal from the man you love most in this world, then you know what the following weeks and months held.

You know the stabbing conflict: wanting to run to the man who has always been the one to comfort you, soothe your hurts, and wipe away your tears, and yet holding back because he is the very person who wounded you in the first place.

You know the numbness which envelopes. You go about your daily routines, trying to bury your emotions for fear of losing control once that floodgate is open.

You know the inward battle between desperately loving this man, and yet contemplating methods of cruel revenge against him. You know the temptations that come out of nowhere, inviting you to betray your husband the way he so heartlessly betrayed you.

You've asked the questions: "Why? Was it my fault? Am I not enough? How could he do this to me?

To us? To his God?" You've asked them so many times, they've even invaded your dreams. You've felt fury, agony, despair, emptiness.

I know the feeling of isolation, like there's no one who understands, no one who will listen to your heart without passing judgment. I know the struggle to balance your desire to protect your husband's reputation with your need to find someone to confide in. I know the suffocating fear that says it's only a matter of time before he betrays you again. I know. I've been there. I'm still there at times.

What I want *you* to know is this:

There is hope for your marriage.

You are Not Alone

> *Blessed be the God and Father of our Lord*
> *Jesus Christ, the Father of mercies and the*
> *God of all comfort, who comforts us in all*
> *our tribulation, that we may be able to*
> *comfort those who are in any trouble, with*
> *the comfort with which we ourselves are*
> *comforted by God (2 Corinthians 1:3-4).*

A portion of this chapter first appeared in 2014 as a post on my personal blog. Since that time, women from all over the country have contacted me to share their stories. Some are inspiring accounts of redemption. Some are heartbreaking stories of relationships destroyed by pornography. One thing is clear. The devastation of pornography is common, even within the Body of Christ.

Statistics suggest that 50% of men who claim to be Christians are addicted to porn.[1] Imagine, then, the number of women who experience the heartache of discovering their husband is virtually cheating on them! Pornography is an ugly, rampant sin that invades marriages everywhere, and it doesn't stop at the doors of the church.

Here's the good news. Countless marriages have recovered from pornography and now bring glory to God. In the early days after Joshua's confession, I sought council from several older couples I respect. I was surprised, and somewhat relieved, to learn that pornography had been a struggle for those couples at one point or another. Surprised because I couldn't imagine such happy couples having a past of unfaithfulness. Relieved because it assured me that we weren't the only ones, and that there was hope that we could still have the marriage God designed for us.

You are one of countless wives struggling to recover from this blow. Other women, just like you, who have gone through the anguish of broken trust, are committed to fight for their marriages.

You are not alone.

There are women who will hold your hand, cry

---

[1] "Porn Stats (2014 edition)." Covenant Eyes. www.covenanteyes.com/resources/download-your-copy-of-the-pornography-statistics-pack/ (accessed October 2, 2018).

with you, pray with you, and give you confidence that healing is possible. There are already people praying for you who may not even know your name. I'm one of them.

Isn't it reassuring to know that others have navigated these waters before you and have survived? Even more consoling is the knowledge that there is One who is always beside you, comforting you in your deepest sorrow. He knows exactly what you are feeling. He knows the weight of your heart, and sympathizes with your crushed spirit. He was watching when this sin first took hold, and He knows how to slay the dragon. Cast your burdens on Him. He cares for you (1 Peter 5:7).

> *For we do not have a High Priest who cannot sympathize with our weaknesses, but was in all points tempted as we are, yet without sin. Let us therefore come boldly to the throne of grace, that we may obtain mercy and find grace to help in time of need (Hebrews 4:15).*

Grace to help in time of need. Isn't that exactly what we need when we face the shattering storms of life? The grace that only God can provide? It will carry you. It will make it possible for you to have a better marriage than you can possibly imagine in this moment. With the strength and grace of the Lord, you can make it through.

There is Help

*Ointment and perfume delight the heart,
and the sweetness of a man's friend gives
delight by hearty counsel (Proverbs 27:9).*

You need help. You picked up this book because Satan has attacked your marriage and you're looking for weapons to fight back with. That takes determination and courage. I am praying this book offers you the hope and help you need to fight effectively. Nonetheless, sometimes words on a page are not enough.

Sister, there is no shame in seeking help. You need counselors who can offer you wisdom and personal support. So much in your heart needs to be released in a safe environment. Let other people in. Pornography is a serious addiction, one from which couples rarely recover on their own. Look to older women and counselors within the Body of Christ who can minister to you while you and your husband face this crisis.

Pornography thrives on secrecy. Because of this, men find it difficult to admit when they struggle. This sense of shame bleeds over to us as wives. We don't want anyone to know that our marriages have difficulties, and we certainly don't want anyone to think badly of our husbands. So we hide our hurt.

Joshua and I are no experts in this field. It has only been just over six years since we began this journey of healing, and we are under no illusions that the battle is over. We aren't writing because we have all the answers, but because there are hundreds of women searching for a sliver of hope. We pray this book offers that hope to you, but we are under no illusion that just reading this book will solve your struggles. Thankfully, God has provided the Body of Christ, full of Christians who are ready to guide and carry you and your husband through your entire journey of healing.

There is Hope

> *Blessed be the God and Father of our Lord Jesus Christ, who according to His abun- dant mercy has begotten us again to a liv- ing hope through the resurrection of Jesus Christ from the dead (1 Peter 1:3).*

Right now you may be wondering if you can ever trust your husband again. You may look at him and wonder what convinced you to entrust your heart to him in the first place. You may not be able to stand the thought of being in the same room, let alone the same bed with him. But know this:

There is hope.

There is forgiveness.

There is healing.

And, eventually, there can be trust.

It is a long, rocky road, and issues you thought you had dealt with may pop up years from now, but in Christ there is hope for your marriage.

> *Love never fails (1 Corinthians 13:8).*

Do you remember why you fell in love with your husband? Can you still list the good qualities in your man? Take out a pen and a piece of paper. I want you to write down the answer to the following question: What do you love about your husband? List as many reasons as possible.

Do it now. I'll wait.

No, seriously, right now.

Done? Okay, good. Now take that piece of paper and hang it up in a place where you'll see it every day. Maybe even somewhere your husband will see it. Go ahead. I'll give you enough time.

Perfect. Now listen. Your husband is still that man. Whether you've been married two years or ten, the qualities you just listed are your husband's character traits. Sure, he's changed some since you first fell in love. Maybe he's a little less romantic. Maybe he's not quite as patient. But he's still the man you married.

Your husband is not his addiction. Pornography does not define him. He's not perfect, but his history of porn use doesn't erase all of his good qualities, either. On those tough days when Satan tries to sow seeds of misery and discontent in your heart, read through that list several times. That is your husband.

My husband is a good, godly man. I truly believe he is the absolute best person in the world for me. He loves, cherishes, protects, encourages, strengthens, and sacrifices for me. He treats me like the most precious gift on earth. But Joshua is just a man. He has moments of weakness, temptation, folly. When the stresses of life are great, sometimes those temptations seem unbearable and he stumbles.

Joshua's sin of pornography was horrific and it shook me to my core. But that's how God feels every time I lie, every time I lose my temper with my children, every time I fail to glorify Him. It hurts my God's heart. I am in no way minimizing the significance of Joshua's sin, but who of us has not struggled against some vice we cannot seem to defeat, a sin which at times seems impossible to overcome?

For all have sinned and fall short of the
glory of God (Romans 3:23).

We all stumble. We all fail. Your husband's struggle with pornography does not mean there is nothing good in him. You married this man for a reason. He's still the man you fell in love with. He's imperfect, he's hurt you beyond words, and he has set your marriage up for years of hardship, but he is still your man. If he is like most husbands struggling with pornography, he wants to be free. He loves you and longs for you both to have the marriage you ought to have.

But God demonstrates His own love toward
us, in that while we were yet sinners, Christ
died for us (Romans 5:8).

We have an opportunity to reflect Christ's love for every undeserving soul. We can choose to demonstrate

His mercy and forgiveness toward our husbands and thwart Satan's attempts to bring shame and reproach upon the Body of Christ. The storms we weather can create stronger marriages—beacons of light in a dark world that dishonors marriage and treats spouses as disposable. We can demonstrate God's grace by the way we choose to cherish and honor our husbands, even when we think they don't deserve it.

Your husband needs you by his side. To help him, you have to turn toward him. This is not easy—in fact, it is incredibly difficult. It is not natural to reopen your heart to the one who piercingly wounded it. To choose to become vulnerable again to the man who shattered your trust goes against everything in human nature. But if you are going to rebuild trust and work toward a God-honoring marriage, you must turn your heart toward your husband. This means allowing him to see your pain.

I went through several different stages of emotions in those first few weeks after Joshua's confession. I truly felt as if something, part of our marriage – part of me – had died. I saw Joshua suffering, knew he was fighting similar feelings of hopelessness and defeat, but I didn't know how to be there for him while I felt so lost.

Slowly, with much encouragement from Joshua, I began verbally expressing my feelings to him, even when the words I said were painful for us both. It's important to communicate your thoughts and feelings. If you try to hide them, they will fester until what was only a feeling becomes your outlook on life.

To rebuild your relationship, you must commit to gentle, open, and honest communication. It's hard. Oh, I know it's hard. But once you both fully commit to healing your relationship, the beautiful (yet difficult) journey begins.

With prayer, counsel, open communication, sheer determination, and the grace of God, your marriage can recover from this shock and become stronger than ever. You can one day look at your husband and see a man cleansed by the power of Christ, a man who loves and adores you, a man you feel blessed to be married to. You can find more purpose, more intimacy, more meaning in your marriage than you ever thought possible.

Believe me.

I've seen the other side of the storm.

Confessions of a Former Porn Addict

Mondays were always hard for me. The spiritual boost I got from Sundays gave me the determination to quit my secret sin. Then Monday rolled around and I went right back—I couldn't leave the pornography alone.

I tried to quit. I made (and broke) promises to God which still haunt me. I threw my computer down, hoping it would break. I even hoped I would just die shortly after crying out in repentance to God—because I knew the whole time I wasn't strong enough to stay clean for long. I thought if God would just allow me to somehow die soon after repenting, maybe I could still make it to heaven.

I wish I had been honest before we were married about how completely addicted I was. Truthfully, I don't think I could have been that vulnerable with Brittany before we were married. Even after we were married, I wasn't close enough to her to open myself up like that. And that lack of closeness meant that, even if I had said something, her pain wouldn't have hurt me enough to get me to quit. Sure, I stopped for a time after we were married, but my lack of honesty left the door open to Satan and closed to Brittany.

I wanted to tell her about my addiction several times before, but I always convinced myself to keep quiet. I almost told her a week before I did. I went to my boss and asked to leave work early, but we were slammed with freight and he couldn't let me off. I should have insisted, since this was far more important than work, but I didn't have the resolve. Satan still had too strong a hold.

The Monday I finally told her, I insisted on leaving work early and actually made it home without chickening out. The whole way home, I was scared, nervous, wanting to overcome this addiction, but scared that I'd never be able to win. I had tried to quit so many times before. I was hoping that somehow Brittany could make this time different. I hoped that maybe if she knew, I could find some way to stop. But I didn't really believe I would. I had no real confidence of ever getting out of pornography. I hated myself for looking, for going back time and time again.

When I told Brittany the truth, I was hopeless, scared, and completely broken. Seeing how I hurt her was more devastating than I could have comprehended. The pain I inflicted on her is one of the things that kept me from falling back into sin when I otherwise would have. I had been lacking a close relationship with God and didn't recognize or care about the pain I caused Him. When I saw Brittany's pain I was devastated. I knew that I hadn't just hurt her, but that I had truly hurt God too. Seeing her pain helped me grow closer to both her and God.

I didn't always know how to love Brittany, but I wanted to. I did stupid things. I broke her trust, I hurt her deeply, and I made her wonder over and over if anything was really going to change. But today, I have been clean for six and a half years. I have a deeper relationship with God and my wife than I ever thought possible. I am purposefully open, not just with Brittany but with everyone. I start the day looking forward to the things I get to accomplish rather than wondering how long I can make it today without looking at porn.

CHAPTER 2:
A CULTURE OF PORN

Ash. Smoke. Lava.

Obliteration.

Perhaps one of the greatest archeological finds of history came in the 18th century, when the excavation of Pompeii enabled historians to glimpse the last moments of a once-thriving Roman city. The discoveries were both astonishing and morbidly fascinating. Bread still in ovens. Games still lying on the street where children once played. Imprints of bodies frozen in time, expressions of horror still etched on their faces. Life, suddenly and unexpectedly, extinguished.

In AD 79, life in Pompeii was full of pleasure. A resort for the wealthy, the city flourished by appealing to the senses, and giving visitors a place to indulge in their passionate desires. Gratification was the quest, and Pompeii held the promise of satisfaction.

Until Mount Vesuvius erupted in an explosion of brutal fury.

The catastrophic event captured a slice of ancient Roman society buried under 14 to 17 feet of pumice. Nearly the entire city of Pompeii was preserved by a blanket of ash, including prominently displayed artwork. Artwork of deplorable content.

Pompeii is widely known for the scandalous frescos and sculptures discovered beneath the volcanic lava. The images were so shockingly obscene that many of the artifacts were locked away by order of King Francis I of Naples. The artifacts were exhibited for public viewing in 2000, but youth remain restricted. Even in an age where sexual license is lauded, it is recognized that such images are abhorrent. And yet, the lust of the eye has been catered to for centuries.

Pornography is nothing new.

Ancient Greece, Early Renaissance Europe, Native America – these cultures were all rife with sexual sin, including the use of imagery to incite sexual fantasies. The historical use of pornography is evident from the art continually discovered from ancient societies. It is also described in written accounts. Pornography is not a new beast. Nor has it been relegated to only the most licentious cultures of history.

The lust of the eye has been a problem ever since the Garden, when Eve saw, took, and ate.

> *So when the woman saw that the tree was*
> *good for food, that it was pleasant to the*
> *eyes, and a tree desirable to make one wise,*
> *she took of its fruit and ate. She also gave*
> *to her husband with her, and he ate*
> *(Genesis 3:6).*

When Eve saw something pleasant to her eyes, something desirable, something that promised to bring her a life of pleasure, she took. She lusted after what was not rightfully hers to enjoy, and it cost her dearly.

Lust has been a problem throughout all ages since. The fight against the lust of the eyes and the lust of the flesh—looking for sexual fulfillment where God never intended it to be found—is a struggle, especially for men.

The Expansion of Pornography

It is commonly quipped that any time we have a new advancement in technology, the first thing that will be broadcast is a verse from the Bible; the second will be something having to do with sex.

With the printing press came the blessing of the wide distribution of the Bible. It was phenomenal! For the first time, the common man could hold the Word of God in his own hands. Unfortunately, it wasn't long before he could also get hold of sordid fiction. During the Victorian era, (commonly thought of as a "prudish" time in England's history), there were more than 50 porn shops on Holywell Street in London, supplying an abundance of erotic material.

Pushing the boundaries of social mores further, the invention of photography led to the development of burlesque portraits and "pin-up girls." By the early 1900s, mass produced posters of scantily clad women adorned the walls of college dorms and military barracks. In the 1930s, hot commodity men's magazines featured "Vargas girls" (named after a popular Peruvian painter who specialized in cartoons of sensual women). By the time World War II rolled around, images of seductive, mostly nude women became an icon of courage. Scared young men were encouraged to look at such photos just before going into battle, as these "inspiring female patriots" promised to impart a "fighting spirit." Soldiers sometimes carried these pictures in their pockets right alongside photographs of their sweethearts back home, or painted copies onto the noses of their fighter jets.

Lines began to blur. In some circles it was considered a girl's patriotic duty to send her beau a racy picture of herself in order to remind him why he was fighting. If pornography was what helped get a guy through the horrors of war, why not let it be a picture of his own girlfriend? What was so bad about a little endorphin-inducing picture anyway? As more and more young people became attracted to the idea of using arousing images to lift spirits, the open display of risqué photos became more accepted in American society.

Photography advanced quickly. At the same time, cinema captivated audiences around the world. Early on, moving pictures were special attractions at carnivals and sideshows; a few seconds of innocent entertainment. Inevitably, someone soon came up with the idea of filming shocking scenes to attract more revenue. The first pornographic film is thought to have been created by a French producer in 1896. Television was subject to government regulations, so pornography did not show up in public broadcasts until much later, but sexual obscenity could be found in films (especially French films) by the turn of the 20th century.

In the 1960s, theaters specifically dedicated to showing pornographic movies popped up around the country. As home videos became accessible, the porn industry grew at an even more alarming rate. VHS tapes could be viewed in the privacy of your own home, where anything you saw, and anything you did, was your own business. Regular video rentals were usually a few bucks each, but rental stores could make more than five times that off a porn video from their adult room.

Porn was paying big.

The digital age dawned. Computers were originally text only, but soon technologic advancements allowed one to upload and download images. One of the very first digital copyright infringement cases involved a company taking old *Playboy* magazines, scanning them in, and charging a fee for a subscription to view the digital images in their systems. The company was making $3.2 million dollars by 1993, just before *Playboy* won the lawsuit. Yes, even before most people had a personal computer in their home, people were fighting over digital porn.

Then along came the internet. The porn industry exploded. Now anyone could upload pictures to the web and connect with people around the world. Small-time virtual porn shops began to populate. With the privacy personal computers afforded, these sites made a killing.

The level of involvement in the "experience" of

pornography was also expanding. Along with the advent of the internet came the two-way, anonymous interaction provided by chat rooms. People could pay to enter chat rooms where women would engage their sexual desires with dirty talk and nude pictures. Similar to dial-in phone sex (which had been around for years), except now you could actually see the person you were paying. When personal web cams brought the average Joe the ability to upload recordings or conduct live conferences, production of porn videos was no longer limited to the porn industry. You could find people anytime, anywhere, eager to swap visual favors for free.

Once upon a time, getting your hands on pornographic material without anyone knowing was much more difficult than it is today. You either had to be brazen enough to buy it yourself, or shameless enough to get it from a friend. Either way, somebody usually knew about the incident, which kept many from participating. These days, the only person who has to know is the person using the porn for his own pleasure.

Never before has there been a time when pornography was so surreptitiously accessible. We live in a day when XXX movies can be downloaded in an instant in the secrecy of your own bedroom. "Softcore" porn is now broadcast on TV across the nation and can be found any time of day, even in perfectly "innocent" programs. Smartphones with their data and apps provide a feasting ground where there is typically zero accountability and all the confidentiality desired. And while there are sites that do still require a fee for viewing, there is an unlimited amount of explicit material available online free of charge, so not even your credit card company has to know.

Effects of Pornography on Society

The aftermath of Mount Vesuvius vividly portrays the devastation of pornography. Lives abruptly destroyed. Once thriving relationships turned to ashes. Healthy marriages buried under thick, suffocating mire. It is a problem that has devoured not only American culture but societies worldwide.

We see so much of it that sometimes we don't even notice. We go to the mall and walk right by the Victoria's Secret posters without a second thought. It never even registers. At least, not usually with us women. Men, on the other hand, seem to have a radar for sexually explicit images. Their eyes and minds are constantly bombarded with temptation on every corner.

Every second of every day, there are over 28,000 internet users viewing pornography.[2] Studies have found that:

- 1 in 5 mobile searches are for pornography[3]
- 35% of all internet downloads are related to pornography[4]

---

[2] "Porn Stats." Covenant Eyes. www.covenanteyes.com/resources/download-your-copy-of-the-pornography-statistics-pack/ (accessed October 2, 2018).

[3] "Pornography Statistics." Covenant Eyes. www.covenanteyes.com/pornstats (accessed September 24, 2018).

[4] www.webroot.com/us/en/resources/tips-articles/internet-

- 24% of Smartphone users admit to having pornographic content on their phones[5]

People often think of porn addiction as a man's problem, and understandably so. 68% of men age 18-30 view pornography at least once a week,[6] but they're not the only ones. 1 in 3 adults browsing porn sites are women, with roughly 9.3 million females viewing pornography every month.[7] Recent studies revealed that at least 20% of religious women are addicted to porn, too.[8] No one is immune.

American society is saturated in pornography. It is a $97 billion global industry,[9] making $13 billion a year in the U.S. alone.[10] That's more than the NFL, NBA, and Major League Baseball put together.[11] And it's

---

pornography-by-the-numbers (accessed September 24, 2018).

[5] Eldred, Lisa. "5 Tips to Accountability on Smartphones." Covenant Eyes. www.covenanteyes.com/2012/04/12/5-tips-to-accountability-on-smartphones (accessed September 24, 2018).

[6] "Porn Stats (2014 edition)." Covenant Eyes. www.covenanteyes.com/resources/download-your-copy-of-the-pornography-statistics-pack/ (accessed October 2, 2018).

[7] "Pornography Statistics." Family Safe Media. www.familysafemedia.com/pornography-statistics/#anchor2 (accessed September 24, 2018).

[8] "Porn Stats." Covenant Eyes. www.covenanteyes.com/resources/download-your-copy-of-the-pornography-statistics-pack/ (accessed October 2, 2018).

[9] Fattah, Geoffrey. "Porn Industry is Booming Globally." Deseret News. www.deseretnews.com/article/660204138/Porn-industry-is-booming-globally.amp (accessed September 24, 2018).

[10] "Pornography Statistics." Family Safe Media. www.familysafemedia.com/pornography-statistics/#anchor2 (accessed September 24, 2018).

[11] Matthews, Anna and Probst, Caroline. "Pornography Facts:

growing. Porn sites receive more traffic than Amazon, Netflix, and Twitter combined.[12] While there are 1.9 million cocaine users, and 2 million heroin users, there are 40 million regular porn users in the U.S.[13]

The Problem with Porn and Relationships

The Bible emphatically condemns lust as a sin of the world.

> *For all that is in the world—the lust of the flesh, the lust of the eyes, and the pride of life—is not of the Father but is of the world (1 John 2:16).*

Lust is of the world, but even secular groups recognize that viewing pornography causes problems. In 2002, the American Academy of Matrimonial Lawyers met and discussed their findings on pornography's role in divorce. According to these lawyers:

- Over 56% of divorce cases in the U.S. involve the obsessive use of pornography
- 68% of divorces involve one party meeting a new lover over the internet

20 That Will Shcok You." Intellectual Takeout. www.intellectualtakeout.org/article/pornography-facts-20-will-shock-you (accessed September 24, 2018).

[12] "Porn Sites Get More Visitors Each Month Than Netflix, Amazon and Twitter Combined." Huffington Post. www.huffingtonpost.com/2013/05/03/internet-porn-stats_n_3187682.html (accessed September 24, 2018).

[13] "Pornography Statistics." Family Safe Media. www.familysafemedia.com/pornography-statistics/#anchor2 (accessed September 24, 2018).

- 33% of cases in the year 2000 cited sexual chat rooms as a factor in the divorce[14]

There were 11,300 hardcore porn films released in 2002. Compare that to the 470 mainstream Hollywood movies released that same year (many of which include high amounts of sexual content). Is anyone surprised that our culture is heavily influenced by porn? The problem is so significant that in 2005 the discussion was brought before the U.S. Senate in the "Hearing on Pornography's Impact on Marriage & the Family." The following excerpt is from the testimony of sociologist Jill Manning.

> Since the advent of the internet, the pornography industry has profited from an unprecedented proximity to the home, work, and school environments. Consequently, couples, families, and individuals of all ages are being impacted by pornography in new and often devastating ways. Although lots of parents work diligently to protect their family from sexually explicit material, research funded by Congress has shown internet pornography to be 'very intrusive.' ... Leading experts in the field of sexual addiction contend on-line sexual activity is a 'hidden public health

---

[14] "The Impact of Pornography on Marital Relationships." The Wishing Wells Counseling Service. www.wishingwellscounseling.com/the-impact-of-pornography-on-marital-relationships (accessed September 24, 2018).

hazard exploding, in part because very few are recognizing it as such or taking it seriously.'[15]

She went on to cite that pornography consumption is associated with:

- Increased marital distress and risk of separation or divorce
- Decreased marital intimacy and sexual satisfaction
- Infidelity
- Devaluation of monogamy, marriage, and child rearing
- Increased appetite for more graphic types of pornography and sexual activity associated with abusive, illegal, or unsafe practices
- An increasing number of people struggling with compulsive and addictive sexual behavior

While the marital bond is the relationship most vulnerable to the effects of pornography, Ms. Manning's testimony also noted that children and adolescents are the most vulnerable audience. Children who are exposed to pornography experience:

- Lasting negative or traumatic emotional responses

---

[15] Testimony of Jill C. Manning, M.S. before the U.S. Congress, Senate, Subcommittee on the Constitution, Civil Rights and Property Rights Committee of Judiciary. *Hearing on Pornography's Impact on Marriage & the Family.* November 9, 2005. www.judiciary.senate.gov

- Earlier onset of first sexual intercourse
- The belief that superior sexual satisfaction is attainable without having affection for one's partner
- The belief that being married and having a family are unattractive prospects
- Increased risk for developing sexual compulsions and addictive behavior
- Increased risk of exposure to incorrect information about human sexuality
- Overestimating the prevalence of less common practices such as group sex, bestiality, or sado-masochistic activity

Ms. Manning concluded her testimony by saying, "I am convinced internet pornography is grooming young generations of Americans in such a way that their chances of enjoying healthy relationships are handicapped."

The Problem with Porn and Violence

Pornography has a devastating effect on the emotional side of relationships, but it doesn't stop there. It also has a disturbing tendency to encourage violent behavior. Our prisons are filled with serial rapists and murderers, many of whom began their lives in normal homes like yours and mine. How did these once-innocent children become adults capable of such unspeakable crimes? According to Ted Bundy, the infamous murderer and rapist of more than thirty women, for many it started with porn. In an interview with Dr.

James Dobson the evening before his execution, Bundy gave this chilling warning.

> I'm no social scientist, and I don't pretend to believe what John Q. Citizen thinks about this, but I've lived in prison for a long time now, and I've met a lot of men who were motivated to commit violence. Without exception, every one of them was deeply involved in pornography – deeply consumed by the addiction. The F.B.I.'s own study on serial homicide shows that the most common interest among serial killers is pornography. It's true...There is no way in the world that killing me is going to restore those beautiful children to their parents and correct and soothe the pain. But there are lots of other kids playing in streets around the country today who are going to be dead tomorrow, and the next day, because other young people are reading and seeing the kinds of things that are available in the media today.[16]

Repeated exposure to pornographic content (especially violent pornography) is associated with increased incidents of physical and verbal abuse, including rape. One study referenced by *Think Progress* suggested that

---

[16] "Fatal Addiction: Ted Bundy's Final Interview." Focus on the Family. www.focusonthefamily.com/media/social-issues/fatal-adiction-ted-bundys-final-interview (accessed September 25, 2018). Transcript posted at Castimonia. https://castimonia.org/wp-content/uploads/2013/01/ted-bundy-interview-transcript1.pdf (accessed September 25, 2018).

roughly one-third of college men would commit rape if they were sure they could get away with it.[17] This mindset is surely influenced by pornography's frequent depiction of rape as an exciting experience for both the man and the woman.

The Problem with Porn and Perspectives

Am I suggesting that everyone who views pornography is destined to become a serial killer or rapist? Not at all. While graphic depictions of violent sexual acts can and do encourage acting out, not everyone who views porn will become a criminal. However, viewing porn does have a negative effect on the way men view and treat women, and this can spiral into imitation of the depictions to which one has been exposed. Viewing porn leads to a lack of empathy and respect for life, less control over strong emotions like anger and depression, and highly unrealistic expectations for sexual encounters.

Neil Malamuth conducted an experiment in which two groups of men were exposed to two depictions of rape. One depiction presented the rape as eventually being enjoyable to the woman (a "positive" outcome). The other depiction presented the much more realistic reaction of the victim being horrified and repulsed by

---

[17] Edwards, Sarah R., Bradshaw, Kathryn A., and Hinsz Verlin B. "Denying Rape but Endorsing Forceful Intercourse: Exploring Differences Among Responders" *Violence and Gender* Volume 1, No. 4 (2014). Cited by Culp-Ressler, Tara. "1 in 3 College Men in Survey Say They Would Rape A Woman if They Could Get Away With

the rape (a negative outcome). The group of men that was first presented with the "positive" depiction of rape perceived the second rape as less harmful than the group that was exposed to the negative depiction first. Those first exposed to the "positive" depiction believed that a higher percentage of women would find rape to be a pleasurable experience.[18]

Porn warps the understanding of normal male and female relationships. Depicting a one-dimensional view of females, porn portrays women as toys with no feelings, merely there to please a man in whatever way he can imagine. It also communicates to women that men are incapable of self-control and, therefore, not responsible for their sexual exploits.

Is This Pornography?

Pornography's negative effects infiltrate all areas of life, eating away at the moral and ethical standards of our country. It has touched nearly every life in the U.S. Because we live in a society so inundated with porn, recognizing it for what it is can be difficult. Everyone seems to have a different definition of what is permissible to view. God calls us to purity of mind (Titus 1:15), which means we must keep our eyes from all sexual impurity. It's important to understand what that includes. Before we talk about how to recover from a

---

[18] "Pornography Exposure Effects." Criminal Justice. http://criminal-justice.iresearchnet.com/forensic-psychology/pornography-exposure-effects/ (accessed September 24, 2018).

spouse's porn addiction, we must understand what we are dealing with. What exactly is "pornography"?

The Definition

The word "pornography" comes from two Greek roots; "porne," meaning "prostitute" and "graphein," meaning "to write." It is "the writing of harlots."

Webster's 1959 Unified Dictionary and Encyclopedia defines pornography as, "Art with obscene or unchaste treatment of subjects."

"Art" is a wide genre that takes diverse forms. Britannica's Encyclopedia defines pornography a little more specifically.

> "The presentation of sexual behavior in books, pictures, films, or other media solely to cause sexual excitement."

That's a pretty good definition. Keep in mind that what is intended to cause sexual excitement and what actually causes sexual excitement can be two different things.

When one has been exposed to sexual promiscuity repeatedly, it starts to become normal. It doesn't evoke the same level of reaction that it once did. Therefore, it is not what actually *causes* sexual excitement that determines what is appropriate. There are people who get no sexual stimulation from watching Kate Winslet's display of herself in *Titanic* because they've seen much worse; such nudity no longer fazes them. Obviously, that fact doesn't make it okay to watch. Pornography is not determined by what raises a person's pulse.

Neither can you determine what is pornographic merely based on an artist's alleged intentions. For instance art, especially Renaissance art, often portrays nude or mostly nude women. Under the legal definition, this is acceptable in public displays and does not fall under the category of "pornography." According to Duhaime's Law Dictionary, pornography is "The portrayal of sexual acts solely for the purpose of sexual arousal." "Art" and "pornography" are distinguished by the idea that art conveys an appreciation for the beauty of the human body, while pornography is meant solely for sexual gratification.

Is this a fair distinction?

My mom used to play a game with us when we were kids that we called, "This isn't That." She would gather random items from around the house and place them in a bag, then we would all sit in a circle. She would reach in the bag and pull out her first item – perhaps a wooden spoon – and say, "This isn't a wooden spoon; this is," for example, "a queen's royal scepter." She would come up with the silliest use for the item she could imagine, and we would all laugh hysterically. Then the item was passed around the circle for each person to try to come up with an even more ridiculous use for it. But, no matter what we called it, when it made its way all around the circle, it was still just a wooden spoon.

Does God approve of the public display of a naked

body as long as it increases our appreciation for His creation? That sounds pretty similar to calling a wooden spoon a "royal scepter." Just because an image does not fall under the dictionary definition of "pornography" – just because it is not intended to cause a sexual reaction – does not necessarily mean it is pure to look upon.

On the flip side, we can't ban everything that causes every person to lust. There is nothing wrong with a picture of a beautiful, modestly dressed woman. A man having trouble controlling his thoughts when he sees that picture does not mean the picture is pornographic. It means that man has a problem with lust. No amount of censorship will eradicate lust from the heart.

So how are we as Christians to define "pornography"? Britannica's definition gives us a pretty good launching pad for our discussion. Again, pornography is defined as "The presentation of sexual behavior in books, pictures, films, or other media solely to cause sexual excitement." This is a reasonable definition if we keep in mind two caveats: (1) Some find sexual arousal in images that are clearly not intended to be pornographic, such as illustrations in a medical textbook, and (2) just because a work isn't *solely* intended for arousal, doesn't mean it is pure and wholesome.

Entertaining Porn

The word "porn" is frequently associated with images (often found online) viewed for sexual pleasure. But pornography is much broader than that.

One common form of pornography—yet rarely

discussed—is the graphic romance novel. The written word can be just as pornographic as an image. It's called "Erotica" – fiction that is written to engage the lustful mind. Here's where women often fall into the trap. Because we usually think pornography means images, and that is just a man's problem, we sometimes excuse other sinful material. In fact, many women fall into the trap of porn addiction without ever even knowing that's what they're looking at because they're viewing the imagery through words rather than pictures.

Perhaps a good working definition of pornography in the context of our discussion is, "Any media (words, images, sculpture, video, sounds, etc.) that, as part of its design or nature, causes sexual arousal for someone or something other than one's spouse." Anything that excites sexual arousal and which does not rightfully belong to you, be it imagery intended for sexual gratification or a lingering lustful look at what was not originally meant to be provocative, is sinful for you to view.

We can call it "entertainment." We can call it "education." We can call it "stress relief" and "innocent fun" and "no big deal." But when we get right down to it, much of what we are invited to view in our society is pornographic, plain and simple.

No matter what you call it, any images that display the human body with the intent to sexually excite viewers are pornographic in nature. It might be dressed up, watered down, or washed out. There may even be a "G" rating. But if there are scenes exhibiting lewd behavior with the aim of stimulating a physical reaction, it's pornography. Let's stop trying to call a wooden spoon a royal scepter!

We wonder why our boys are addicted from such young ages, why 9 and 10 year old children are acting out sexually. We shake our heads in disgust over the industry that makes its millions off of young girls and hopeless men. And then we sit down in our comfy recliners, flip on the TV, and watch an episode of *Game of Thrones*.

What do we expect?

We live in a culture of sexual depravity, partly because we refuse to call sin "sin." We call it "entertainment." We say, "It doesn't have that much in it…" We say, "Watching bedroom scenes doesn't really affect me like that." No? It should. In healthy individuals, the sight of two people making love should cause us to blush and turn away! It should bother you. It should make you uncomfortable. And if it doesn't, it's not because you're a girl and "girls aren't visual." It's because you've been desensitized.

We cannot excuse nudity for the sake of entertainment. It's not just a sweet chick flick or a thrilling action movie. When it's got features that bring sexual pleasure, the temptation to lust, or a display of the human body for entertainment, that's pornography—and it's not okay. It's disgusting.

We've got to be aware of just how pervasive porn is, even in what are supposed to be family-friendly forms of entertainment. One night after a three-month hiatus from movies and television, Joshua and I decided to relax with an innocent sounding animated film. We were shocked by how much filth was presented in this "children's" cartoon. It is amazing how much junk you miss when you're used to seeing it all the time, but when you give yourself a reset you get a fresh perspective.

When we talk about inappropriate films, we're not only talking about R-rated movies. We're talking about movies nearly everyone accepts as perfectly innocent. We're talking about movies like *The Little Mermaid* (why is it okay for us to watch Ariel transform into a naked human?). We've got to be more aware of what we're viewing.

Whether it's books, movies, pictures, artwork, music, or any other form of media, you need to ask: is this exhibiting sinful actions? This is a question we must all consider, not just our husbands. How can we as Christians find enjoyment from the very sins which made it essential for Christ to sacrifice His life? Is your entertainment glorifying sins that sent Christ to the cross?

God clearly condemns sexual immorality and despises the glorification of such sins. He allows us the freedom to choose what we want to view, but make no mistake about it—our entertainment choices absolutely have the power to separate us from God. Never from His love, but from the fellowship we should have with Him.

*And even as they did not like to retain God
in their knowledge, **God gave them over** to
a debased mind, to do those things which
are not fitting; being filled with all unrighteousness, sexual immorality, wickedness,
covetousness, maliciousness; full of envy,
murder, strife, deceit, evil-mindedness; they
are whisperers, backbiters, haters of God,
violent, proud, boasters, inventors of evil
things, disobedient to parents, undiscern-
ing, untrustworthy, unloving, unforgiving,
unmerciful; who, knowing the righteous
judgment of God, that those who practice
such things are deserving of death, not only
do the same **but also approve of those who
practice them** (Romans 1:28-32,
emphasis mine).*

It hardly needs to be stated, but pornography is a
sin. Satan would have us believe porn is a harmless bite
of forbidden fruit; a way of enjoying the pleasures of
sin without actually engaging in the act. He uses such
tactics to convince men that receiving pleasure from
looking at a woman is not the same as actually committing the sin of sexual immorality. God says otherwise.

*You have heard that it was said to those of
old, 'You shall not commit adultery.' But I
say to you that whoever looks at a woman
to lust for her has already committed adul-*

tery with her in his heart
(Matthew 5:27-28).

The Lord speaks vehemently against those who
have "eyes full of adultery" and who convince others
that sin is not really sin.

> *But these, like natural brute beasts made to*
> *be caught and destroyed, speak evil of the*
> *things they do not understand, and will ut-*
> *terly perish in their own corruption, and*
> *will receive the wages of unrighteousness,*
> *as those who count it pleasure to carouse in*
> *the daytime. They are spots and blemishes,*
> *carousing in their own deceptions while*
> *they feast with you, **eyes full of adultery***
> *and that cannot cease from sin, enticing*
> *unstable souls. They have a heart trained in*
> *covetous practices, and are accursed chil-*
> *dren (2 Peter 2:12-14, emphasis mine).*

All forms of pornography must be rejected, regardless of cultural standards or labels. Sexualized entertainment is contrary to the will of God. Let's be careful
to keep our eyes open to subtle presentations of pornography.

Why?

Pornography is not a new sin. Our society is infest-
ed with its filth. It's everywhere, and it destroys hearts
and souls. It always has. But you, more than most,
know this. With the revelation of your husband's porn

addiction, you now see it everywhere. Your sensitivity to the problem has been ignited, and you can see how even in the church we've allowed ourselves to become desensitized.

After discovering a spouse's unfaithfulness, it is normal to develop an intense aversion to anything that even borders on being sexually provocative. As you have probably found, pornography is painfully difficult to avoid. With such availability, expecting your husband to break his addiction can feel unrealistic. It's not. It's entirely possible for him to conquer this addiction.

The burning question for most wives at this point is: "Why?" Why does your husband look at porn? What's so appealing about it? What can a picture offer him that you can't, and, most importantly, what's it going to take to help him get rid of his addiction and heal your marriage?

Confessions of a Former Porn Addict

Pornography is a slippery thing to define, and I applaud my wife for tackling the difficult task. Pornography has two points of creation, the propagator and the consumer. There is the material created for the purpose of inciting lust, then there is everything else one can choose to lust over.

As someone fighting to no longer be a consumer, I have to admit that I could have consumed nearly anything in a pornographic manner. When you are accustomed to looking so regularly and intently for sexual arousal, cutting off all avenues is incredibly difficult. It's easy to say you are staying away from the sources, while still using seemingly innocent things in the same evil way.

The opportunity is everywhere. It's on the shampoo advertisements, the signs hanging from the ceiling in Wal-Mart, the neighbor's wife who doesn't know what clothing is for, your child's biology textbook, the local community college flyer that came in the mail, the book to help a man stop looking at porn that talks so explicitly about a woman's body that he can't help but imagine the details. Just about anything can be used for illicit pleasure.

Our society is flooded with indecent images. When I became determined to break my addiction, I soon realized that it was impossible to avoid everything that tempted me to lust. Whether those things were intentionally put there to cause me to stumble, or whether the material was created with innocent intentions, I knew I was going to see things that triggered temptation. What I also knew, though, was that the temptation is not the crime. It is when I allow my eyes to linger and my thoughts to turn to lust that I have fallen back into sin. I can't control everything that comes into my view, but I can control how I view it.

CHAPTER 3:
WHAT'S HIS PROBLEM?

When John wrote Revelation to the seven churches of Asia, the three biggest problems he addressed were apathy, false doctrines, and sexual sin. I would not be surprised to see these three sins at the top of the list if he were addressing the church in America today. Lost zeal, twisted Gospel truths, and sexual immorality plague our congregations. All three are treacherous, but sexual sin seems to be particularly difficult to address. It hides well, even among the most respected leaders of the church.

I spoke with a professional counselor recently about how many marriages are struggling as a result of porn addiction. She told me, "90% of couples who have come into my office in the last 3-5 years have come here because of pornography. You would be shocked by who all is doing it."

It seems everywhere you turn, you hear of marriages failing due to infidelity. Perhaps the most common form of infidelity, pornography, has led to the demise of thousands of marriages. According to a Barna Group survey of men, 79% of 18-30 year olds, 67% of 31-49 year olds, and 49% of 50-68 year olds say they view porn at least once a month.[19] It should come as no

---

[19] "Porn Stats." Covenant Eyes.
www.covenanteyes.com/resources/download-your-copy-of-the-

surprise, then, that porn addiction is a factor in over half of the cases of divorce. But what led all of these husbands (and sometimes wives) to this point? How did your husband come to have this problem to begin with?

There are five commonly accepted stages of porn addiction:

1. Early exposure
2. Addiction
3. Escalation
4. Desensitization
5. Sexually Acting Out

Early exposure refers to the first time your husband was introduced to pornography. The average age of first exposure is 8-11 years old. [20] The younger a boy is introduced, the stronger his addiction is likely to become, and the more difficulty he will have in his relationships with women. Ask your husband about the first time he was introduced to porn. This honest look into his personal history will be beneficial to both of you in understanding what led to his addiction.

Many children are introduced to pornography in their own homes, often accidently stumbling across it online while completing homework assignments. Others are introduced by friends who share the images on the school bus, or pass around pictures on the play-

---

pornography-statistics-pack/ (accessed October 2, 2018).

[20] "Consider This." Novus Project. www.thenovusproject.org/resource-hub/parents (accessed September 25, 2018).

ground. All it takes is a single glimpse to spark natural curiosity, leading to undercover investigation.

That's what happened to William. William was a boy full of curiosity. Like most young children, he wanted to know everything there was to know about the world around him. So, when he overheard his parents discussing his older brother's problem with what they called "porn," he had questions. What was porn, and why was his brother so interested in it? As soon as possible, William took to the family computer to ask Google. A few clicks and he was hooked.

At first, William only searched for pornography every few days; just whenever he had some free time and he happened to be home alone. Before he knew it, he was obsessing over the images he viewed. He thought about them all day during school. He stopped going to friends' houses in the afternoons because he couldn't wait to get home and flip on the computer under the guise of "doing homework." He even dreamed about the parade of seductive women he found. It didn't take long before he had developed a physically felt need for pornography and the sexual pleasure it brought. He was irritable, got frequent headaches, slept poorly, and lost interest in anything but his secret investigations. There was no doubt that he was addicted.

The problem grew. William found himself hungering for increasingly warped content. Addiction leads to escalation as the viewer feels compelled to consume images in greater quantities with more edgy content. In the escalation stage, the user begins to view things that would have repulsed him in the beginning. He seeks shocking, disturbing images in an effort to attain an even greater high. William loathed himself for the things he viewed, but his desire was out of control. He wanted more and more.

This is where desensitization comes into play. As the insatiable hunger for greater stimulation grows, the original images lose their ability to bring that same level of satisfaction. Like William, many men find they need an added shock value to get the same level of excitement they first found. The "soft" stuff isn't doing it anymore. In a marriage relationship, desensitization due to porn may mean that a husband no longer finds fulfillment in his sexual relations with his wife. Frustrated by this, he may withdraw from his wife and immerse himself in more grotesque forms of pornography. All of this leads to the final stage of sexually acting out what one has viewed. This can be in the form of having an affair, perpetrating sexual abuse, hiring a prostitute, or any manner of escalating sexual perversion.

William's story is familiar to many men, many of whom became addicted before they even understood the anatomy of the human body. All it takes is a split second of unintended exposure and the idle curiosity of a child can lead him to destruction. Thankfully, William found help before reaching the stage of acting out what he saw. But he continues to face the reality of just how far his desensitization took him, especially now that he is seeing the long-term effects on his marriage.

The Struggle with Nature

With over half of the male population in our country struggling with an addiction to porn, it is no surprise that marriages all around us are crumbling due in large part to this sexual sin. But, why? What is it that draws your husband to images of fake women even if you have made your body available to him? Why does he feel uncontrollably attracted to a screen full of unrealistic portrayals of sex when he has access to fulfilling, God-ordained intimacy with you?

Before we answer that question, we need to first have a basic understanding of how God created men. Specifically, that (a) men tend to be more visually stimulated than women, and (b) men generally have a higher sex drive than women. Although these are certainly generalities, appreciating these common differences between men and women helps us understand why pornography is so appealing.

Men are Visual

I know you've heard it a thousand times, but it's true. Men are, in general, much more visually stimulated than women. "I can't take my eyes off of you" isn't just sweet nothings. A woman's naked body is a magnet to a man's eyes. It can feel impossible for him to turn his eyes away from a display of womanly curves. God designed men to be strongly attracted to the appearance of a woman's body, and that is a pure ingredient of marriage.

Solomon speaks eloquently of the visual pleasure

he found in his bride, "Your two breasts are like two fawns, twins of a gazelle, which feed among the lilies. Until the day breaks and the shadows flee away, I will go my way to the mountain of myrrh and to the hill of frankincense" (Song of Solomon 4:5-6). Visual stimulation is part of God's plan. Unfortunately, because of sin in the world, this also means it is a challenge for men to bounce their eyes away from women who do not belong to them, especially in a society where the presentation of flesh abounds.

Everywhere you look you see skin. Cleavage, midriffs, thighs; these aspects of a woman's body are accentuated in our culture for the purpose of attracting the gaze of men, and frankly many women enjoy the attention. What many ladies fail to realize is that by wearing tight, short, thin apparel to bring attention to their bodies, they are tempting a man to destroy his soul.

Not only are men visually stimulated, but what is less understood by the female population is that men have an uncanny ability to instantly recall images they have viewed only once – even those viewed decades ago. My husband can still vividly remember the picture that introduced him to the details of a woman's body. He was just a boy when he saw it, but the image is burned into his mind and is something he must choose to forget even now.

Being exposed to images of naked women or depictions of lewd behaviors ignites desire and promises easy access to sexual satisfaction. These images can stick with a man and pop up unexpectedly, enticing a return to the pleasure of pornography even after he has been clean for years.

Men have a High Sex Drive

Generally speaking, men have a higher libido than women. On average, men think about sex roughly four times as much as women. While women generally gain greater satisfaction from emotional connections with their husbands, men feel most connected with their wives through sex. This is why emotional affairs are more of a temptation for women, while visual affairs are a stronger lure for men.

Men are aroused more easily than women, and they take a more direct route to sexual satisfaction. While a woman's arousal may change depending on mood, atmosphere, time of month, or whether her husband remembered to take the garbage out, a man is ready for sex at almost any given moment. It can take a woman more than 45 minutes of foreplay to be ready to make love, but a man can go from zero to 60 in a matter of seconds. These differences in nature can keep things interesting, but they require us to be patient with one another and learn specifics about how to satisfy each other. They are differences which Satan loves to use as weaknesses.

Whereas God designed the marriage bed to be an exciting dance between two lovers, selfishness can turn it into a hostile battleground. A wife's lower libido may make it tempting for her to discourage her husband's advances, while a husband's high sex drive can make him impatient with his wife's slower response to his wooing. The ensuing frustration can lead to temptation for both parties.

When either the husband or the wife feels their needs are being overlooked, temptation arises to seek fulfillment in other ways. For wives, that might mean seeking emotional connection and attention from other men. For husbands, their high sex drive and desire for sexual satisfaction might mean seeking illicit gratification.

Vance Hutton said in his talk on pornography at Polishing the Pulpit in 2017, "What is so honorable within marriage becomes a matter of condemnation outside of marriage."[21] It is the very nature God gave us which Satan twists into a sinful pursuit of self-indulgence. While God created us to enjoy a satisfying physical relationship with our spouse, Satan tempts us with the promise that we can find sexual fulfillment from sources outside of marriage.

Because men are apt to have the higher sex drive, addiction to sexual gratification tends to be a greater temptation for men than for women. Satan wants to persuade your husband that he can find a heightened level of excitement in the bodies of other women—whether he feels satisfied in his physical relationship with you or not.

---

[21] Hutton, Vance. "Eight Harmful Effects of Pornography and 'Is Pornography Sexual Immorality?'" Polishing the Pulpit 2017.

The Porn Appeal

Understanding how God wired our men can help us understand why pornography is such a strong temptation, but obviously God didn't create men to give into that temptation. He intends us to find sexual fulfillment in the marriage union. When that union is functioning properly, the level of satisfaction is unmatched by digital sex. So, if a man has access to this satisfying physical relationship in marriage, what makes porn so appealing?

Instant Gratification

A lack of patience and a desire to instantly satisfy a strong sex drive is often what leads men into the path of pornography. Pornography is a completely selfish, me-centered pursuit. It is entirely self-serving, and doesn't require a man to give anything at all. With a few clicks and some time alone, a man can satisfy his sexual cravings without concern for the woman he's using—no fear of getting her pregnant, and no responsibility to give anything of himself. He can explore every sexual interest he has without pausing to consider what would please the woman on the screen.

God created sex to involve two people. It is a gift to both the husband and the wife, and is most fulfilling when both are focused on pleasing the other, keeping the principle of Philippians 2:3-4 in mind.

> *Let nothing be done through selfish ambition or conceit, but in lowliness of mind let each esteem others better than himself. Let*

> *each of you look out not only for his own*
> *interests, but also for the interests of*
> *others.*

Sex is to be a passionate expression of love between a husband and wife, not merely a chance to attain sexual release (although that is a wonderful side effect). It is an incredibly rewarding experience when both partners pay attention to the desires of the other and pour themselves out in an effort to deepen their spouse's pleasure.

Pornography is just the opposite. It is an expression of self-love. Instead of focusing on how to please your spouse, your only concern is how to please yourself. With no expectations placed on him from the girl on the computer screen, a man immerses himself completely in his own passions without regard to the feelings of anyone else.

Pornography is easy. Porn doesn't say no because of a headache, it doesn't have complicated feelings, and it doesn't require patience. Instant gratification is attractive, especially when your sexual desire is constantly in high gear. There is no waiting for the computer to be in the right mood. The most warming up you have to do is turning on your device. Porn offers unrestricted access to instantaneous sexual pleasure. Some husbands even convince themselves this is actually a good way to handle their need for an outlet. "At least I'm not sleeping around or bugging her for sex all the time."

This instant gratification is especially appealing

when a man does not receive frequent sexual release through intimacy with his wife. Denying himself the pleasure of easily achieving release through porn and masturbation is a difficult standard to meet when a man has no other means of satisfaction. This is an area where wives bear some responsibility. 1 Corinthians 7 commands husbands and wives not to deprive each other in their physical relationship because of the door it opens for temptation. I almost hate to mention this fact because too many women already feel as if it is their fault their husbands look at porn. That's not what I am saying. You did not force your husband to look at pornography by not having enough sex with him. It's not as if he simply had to find release somewhere, and porn was the only option. No. Sexual pleasure and release are to be found in the marriage bed alone. Men are not beasts without control over their sexuality. However, I am saying it is much more difficult for a man to stay away from pornography when his physical needs are not being met at home.

> *Nevertheless, **because of sexual immorali-**
> **ty**, let each man have his own wife, and let
> each woman have her own husband. Let the
> husband render to his wife the affection due
> her, and likewise also the wife to her hus-
> band. The wife does not have authority over
> her own body, but the husband does. And
> likewise the husband does not have authori-
> ty over his own body, but the wife does. **Do**
> **not deprive one another** except with con-*

sent for a time, that you may give your-
selves to fasting and prayer; and come to-
*gether again **so that Satan does not tempt***
you because of your lack of self-control
(1Corinthians 7:2-5, emphasis mine)

God commands husbands and wives to give their bodies to one another, because He knows that a lack of sexual release invites temptation. There are legitimate reasons and seasons when your sexual relationship with your husband might ebb. Pregnancy and childbirth are commonly straining times on a couple's sex life. Morning sickness, hormones, and new routines may demand that the usual frequency of sex be temporarily suspended. The period after having a baby can be an especially long season. Your body needs plenty of time to heal after going through the marathon of giving birth. Exhaustion from adjusting to the erratic sleep patterns of a newborn makes it seemingly impossible to find an opportunity for romance. Not to mention, a woman's postpartum hormones often cause low libido and a rollercoaster of emotions which make it difficult for her to get in the mood.

Other times of life that may cause a dip in your sexual relationship are major life changes such as a move, a new job, menopause, or a medical emergency. Those are legitimate reasons for lower sexual activity than you would normally experience in your marriage. However, we need to be sure we are not simply finding excuses not to give our husbands what they need physically.

Your body is not your own. It belongs to your husband and you are responsible for making yourself available to meet his needs. While a husband also has the responsibility to be patient with his wife and understanding of her limitations, wives must think of their husband's needs before their own. That's what sacrificial love is about. When life gets busy and a wife does not pay attention to the physical relationship she shares with her husband (or lack thereof), a husband is left in frustration, wondering if they will ever get back to a satisfying amount of sex.

Now, please don't shut down. Say it with me, "A lack of sex is not an excuse to look at porn." It is not your fault that your husband sinned and broke his covenant before God to keep his eyes for you alone. But let's be real and honest here, too. When a husband is constantly rejected by his wife and his attempts at physical intimacy are brushed off, he is vulnerable to temptation and may feel like she is actually pushing him towards it. He is wired to crave sexual release. His emotional, mental, and physical health depends greatly on how satisfied he is with his sex life. Your willingness to offer your body to your husband at any time goes a long way toward keeping temptation at bay.

Escapism

As Joshua will tell you later on, a lack of sex can make a guy go absolutely bonkers. He doesn't think straight. This leads to poor decisions and a less guarded mind. Interestingly, however, frequency of sex is not always a complaint among men who view pornography.

"I just don't understand," Brenda vents. "I've always made it a point to make my body available to him. I've never told him, 'No.' I do my best to keep things fun and turn up the heat with lingerie and new things to try. He's got as much opportunity for sex in our marriage as he could possibly want! What gives?"

This irony took William by surprise, too. As a single guy, he assumed his struggle with pornography would end, or at least lessen, once he had a legitimate way to fulfill his sexual needs. But temptation only increased after marriage. He couldn't understand it. He loved Brenda, she never withheld her body from him, and they enjoyed a very fulfilling sex life. But he couldn't quit the porn.

This is because porn is not necessarily about sex. William and Brenda are newlyweds who saved sex for their wedding night. They revel in the gift of pure intimacy in marriage. When asked if he felt he needed more sex, William laughed and said, "I'm not sure I could take much more!" It wasn't a lack of sex that drove William to the computer screen.

It was a desire for escape.

As much as he loved their life together, marriage was still a big adjustment for William. Sharing his home with another person after years of solitude was occasionally irritating and he craved a way of escape from the new responsibilities of being a husband. Pornography opened her arms wide.

Escapism is a common reason men turn to porn. In fact, it was a huge contributing factor in Joshua's addiction after marriage. Our life was crazy busy, with lots of big changes in those first two years. Two babies before our second anniversary was enough to overwhelm us both. Add to that the stress of financial insecurity, a major change in life plans, and a wife who was struggling with post-partum hormones and you had a recipe that invited disaster. Joshua, an introvert by nature, found it difficult to engage in our increasingly chaotic life. He was exhausted and wanted a method of relaxation that didn't require anything from him. Stress, hardships in marriage, and feeling overwhelmed made the fantasy world of pornography all the more appealing.

Low Self-Esteem

Low self-esteem is a large part of why many men seek porn. Particularly true of men who grew up in homes with abusive fathers, men who have poor self-image are more likely to succumb to the embrace of pornography. Psychological scars from childhood or past relationships can leave a man unwilling to risk the vulnerability of exposing his own weaknesses. He turns to the ever-ready girls on the porn stage rather than risk opening up to his wife. Shame, low self-esteem, and guilt often drive a man to find comfort in porn. These feelings also keep him hooked because he is afraid that if he admits his struggle, his wife will lose all respect she has for him and, once again, he will see himself as worthless.

Some men find that they prefer porn to sex because it covers their inadequacies. If a guy feels inadequate at pleasing his wife sexually, this can cause him to think poorly of himself. He may seek to soothe a fear of failure by simply avoiding the bedroom and getting his sexual release from his own imagination. A man doesn't have to prove anything to a screen. He doesn't have to worry about being worthy of respect. The girl on the screen looks back at him with eyes full of admiration. He knows it's fake, but when he sees her expression he can fantasize that it's especially for him, that he is a big shot worthy of those appreciative glances. Especially during times when a husband feels like he's failing in other areas, porn seems to promise undivided respect and attention.

Men who experienced sexual abuse as a child may also find it difficult to be vulnerable with their wives in their physical relationship. Sexual abuse damages one's view of sexuality, creating a sense of shame over even legitimate pleasure. It may cause a man to feel embarrassment over physical contact, even with his wife. Pornography feels safer. It makes him feel as if he is in complete control of what is happening to him. The low self-esteem which results from a history of abuse is eased by the feeling of power gained from viewing porn.

Instant gratification, escapism, and low self-esteem make it more tempting for a man to look at pornography. Recognizing those factors helps us understand why our men fall into porn addictions. But they do not ultimately answer our primary question.

Why does your husband look at porn?

It's not just because he's stressed. Plenty of people under high levels of stress do not turn to porn. It's not just because he had a difficult past. That might help you sympathize with how strong the temptation to self-medicate can be, but it doesn't really explain why he finds relief in porn. It's not just because he's not getting enough sexual fulfillment from his wife. Plenty of men are able to go for long periods without sex and withstand the lure of pornography. So, why does a man look at pornography?

The answer is: Lust.

Lust

God gave man a natural desire to enjoy the beauty of his wife's body. Satan twists that natural inclination into a perverted, self-seeking desire to feast his eyes upon all female bodies in order to indulge an inordinate craving for sexual pleasure. In other words, Satan takes the gift of visual pleasure God gave men to be enjoyed in marriage and turns it into self-gratifying lust.

Lust is the "unlawful desire of carnal pleasure... to desire eagerly the gratification of carnal appetite" (Noah Webster's 1828 Dictionary of American English). In the case of a man lusting after a woman's body, it is the eager longing to gratify his sexual appetite in an illegitimate way.

Proverbs 6:25 contains a father's warning to his son against finding pleasure in a seductress, "Do not lust after her beauty in your heart, nor let her allure you with her eyelids." She may promise respect, admiration, and satisfaction, but she will lead only to destruction.

Lust is a breach of God's law, with serious repercussions. It has no place in the heart of a Christian, yet it is one of the most common struggles among men today. Like the call of a siren promising pleasure without consequence, pornography lures men into her lair by appealing to the natural instinct God gave them. Offering an unlimited supply of bodies (with endless variety), porn draws the gaze of over 40 million users in the U.S. alone. Unguarded eyes are a given in the world, but they should not be an attribute of the Body of Christ.

It is possible for Christian men to control their sexual longings and to channel those desires toward their wives alone. God expects this. Job made a solemn pledge in Job 31:1. "I have made a covenant with my eyes; why then should I look upon a young woman?" Job was so committed to keeping a tight rein on his fleshly desires that he made a vow before God that he would not indulge in lust. He would not permit himself to glance longingly after the body of a woman who did not belong to him. All Christian men should have this same covenant with God not to look with lust upon any woman.

How Can He?

How can he claim to love me and look at all these naked women? He says it has nothing to do with how he feels about me, but I don't understand that. He can't love me while also loving to look at porn!

Rachel's stress level had skyrocketed since finding out about her husband's porn use. The desperation in her voice was clear when she phoned me one afternoon to pour out her misgivings about the viability of her marriage. She wondered if anything she had believed about her relationship with James was true. Nothing was what it had seemed. She questioned everything he had done over the last year. Every happy memory was tainted by the question, "Was he looking at porn even then?" Situations that had seemed a little off were suddenly clicking. It made sense now that he so intently encouraged her to go to bed before him and insisted he didn't need as much sleep. It was now clear why he seemed so jumpy whenever she arrived home from work earlier than expected. Things which she had shrugged off at the time now became glaring indications of just how long her husband had been addicted to porn.

It's like I have no idea who he really is or what he's capable of. Just how dark do his obsessions get?

When trust in a marriage has been destroyed, it's normal to feel like everything you thought was true about your husband is a lie. What you know about his character clashes with the knowledge that he is drenched in heinous lust. The idea that he could love you and yet be unfaithful to the most basic principle of your relationship (that sexual gratification belongs in marriage alone), is incomprehensible. You have doubts about every aspect of your marriage. What else has he lied about? Was there ever a time when he was faithful? Doesn't he realize what this does to you? Does he even want to be married anymore? Every proclamation of commitment now sounds like a hollow deception.

Men are particularly good at compartmentalization. Their lives are easily divided into neat little boxes. They have their "work" box, their "family" box, their "social" box, and these boxes can be kept nicely separated in their minds. They have a tendency to be one-tracked, focused on the task at hand without distractions from multitasking or worrying about what will take place in their next box of life. Men are much better than women about living in the present. They are able to leave their work life at the office and come home to their family life, and the two worlds don't often mix. Compartmentalization is not always bad, but sin is able to take any positive and turn it into something destructive.

When a man looks at porn, he disengages from other areas of his life. It's like the world ceases to exist, and all that matters is the pleasure he is experiencing. When he's in his wife's presence he can, to a degree, "forget" about his sin and go on interacting with her as if nothing happened. A Christian man does of course struggle with his conscience, but it is relatively easy to hush his inner voice and step back into his double life in stride. He doesn't allow himself to consider how it is affecting anyone else. This is, by the way, where the "porn doesn't hurt anyone" myth comes from. The correlation between the pleasure that is happening in private and the pain that it causes others just doesn't click. He may not even realize his porn use affects you at all, and may not understand why you feel like your relationship is over. To him, there is a total disconnect.

When your husband insists his porn use has nothing to do with how he feels about you, he's most likely saying what he believes to be true. What he's saying is that it's not your fault. It's not because you gained 20 lbs. It's not because you are too busy for him. It's because he allowed himself to become addicted. It doesn't mean he thinks you are garbage, or that you just can't please him. To him, his love for you and his addiction to porn have nothing to do with each other. They are different boxes in his life.

While these boxes may be separated in your husband's mind, they are not separated in reality. Not in God's eyes. How a man acts at the office must be consistent with how he acts at home because all of his life must be consistent with his Christianity.

Rachel was right. Her husband couldn't truly love her—putting her first at all times—while also loving to look at porn. One cannot love the darkness while walking in the Light (1 John 1:6-7). Walking in the Light – loving with a biblical love – means shunning evil.

James had a weak commitment to Rachel, and he did not love her with a godly love. In Chapter 8, we'll see how this lack of commitment and love continued to play out in their marriage.

When your husband looks at porn, he is not loving you as he should. His actions are inconsistent with the commitment love demands. By allowing lust to rule in his heart, he has separated himself from God and from the proper relationship he should have with you. While this doesn't mean that everything about your marriage is a lie, or that nothing he ever said about caring for you is true, it does mean that his love has been skewed. In the next chapter we'll look at the high price he has paid in trading love for pleasure, and how he has created an addiction that is as difficult to break as an addiction to cocaine.

Confessions of a Former Porn Addict

I remember the first image I ever saw of a completely nude woman. My family and I sat down to watch a movie my mother thought she had seen years before. It wasn't what she remembered. This was a pornographic movie that simply had the same title. Less than five minutes into the movie there was a fully nude woman standing in front of my ten year old eyes. It was immediately turned off and I believe I saw the image for less than one full second, but the fire of interest was lit.

I went looking to find out if that is really what

women look like or if they had altered the image, for surely they wouldn't put a truly nude woman on the screen. My interest led me to start looking at ads that came in the paper; women in swimsuits, undergarments, or just skimpy outerwear. Although it was fun to go looking, those women weren't naked and my questions weren't answered. Then I realized science books were the ticket. Surely biology would give me all the answers I sought. And it did for a time, but then more questions were raised which the book didn't satisfy. Little did I know I had entered a world that knows no satisfaction.

One day while on the computer I began to wonder if it was really that easy to access all the bad stuff people said was on there. It was. Now all my questions were answered. By then I was about sixteen, and I discovered exactly where to find all sorts of sexually interesting things with no limit. I was unprepared to withstand the temptation, and gave in with less resistance than Austria offered Nazi Germany. I was hooked and had no idea how to stop.

The next 11 years were a rollercoaster of trying to quit (and making it a whole week when I was really strong), then going back to porn and hating myself even more. I desperately tried and thought of all sorts of ways to quit, but my addiction was escalating. Sometimes I thought that if I shocked myself enough with how far I went, then maybe that would jolt me awake and I would finally stop. When nothing worked, I just dove deeper. If I couldn't stop, I might as well see if there was more enjoyment waiting. I reasoned that maybe, if I got deep enough, I'd finally silence my conscience and stop hating myself. But I only managed to shut it up for weeks at a time, never a permanent shut down. My parents and other spiritual guides had instilled too much of God's Word in me over the years to allow my conscience to be fully seared. I am so grateful.

As my addiction was escalating, so was my depression. Fear of what my parents would go through is about all that kept me from suicide. I was okay with my family living with me dead (I figured that was better than having a son go where this was inevitably taking me), so I toyed with ways to kill myself without it looking like suicide. Turns out that took more imagination than I had. So, instead of suicide, I started just being stupid. I didn't care how dangerous something was. The more dangerous the better. Maybe I could die and not have to commit suicide. I knew I was going to hell when I died but, hey, starting eternity in hell a couple years early wasn't really going to make much difference. I was going to hell anyway. Nothing could stop that anymore.

Then Brittany came into my life and I saw a flicker of hope. Like many guys, I thought marriage would solve my porn problem. It didn't. Marriage merely became another compartment in my life.

How could I do this to Brittany, the woman I loved and shared life and children with? By loving her, but keeping her in her compartment—not allowing her full access to all of me. I loved her "here in this spot." Her compartment intersected most compartments of my life, but not all. There were places she was not allowed. Those were my secret places, the ones I would sometimes speak of but always in past tense. No one needed to know these secrets were still reality. Only I knew those compartments existed.

I viewed pornography while Brittany and I were married, knowing that I did love her and that it would hurt her, but not knowing how to stop. In my mind, I was doing it against my will. I could not stop looking at, fantasizing about, reading about, and wanting more illicit sexual gratification. So, I was forced to have a compartment for pornography because it would destroy my family if I didn't have a safe place to keep it locked away.

When I told Brittany I loved her, and my porn use had nothing to do with her, I wasn't saying she shouldn't be hurt or that it was all okay. I was trying to impress upon her the reality of the cliché, "It's not you, it's me." I knew it hurt her, I knew it hurt us, but she was in no way the cause or even a contributing factor.

Sometimes I would blame my pornography use on Brittany. I sometimes felt like we weren't having enough sex. Especially early in our marriage, when I felt like sex wasn't forth coming my thinking became clouded and nonsensical. *She never wants sex. She'd prefer I go please myself. And anyway, masturbation would help me think straight again.* I had a hard time convincing myself that not everything sexually pleasurable that came to mind was right. I truly believed that "satisfying my needs" without bothering Brittany was better for her. What I had to learn was to keep my view upon God and be sure I kept God's standard.

There is never any justification for sin. My addiction had nothing to do with Brittany. It wasn't because things were missing in my marriage. It was because I chose to sin. I wanted a close relationship with my wife, a deep relationship with my Creator, along with finding gratification wherever I could. That just doesn't work.

CHAPTER 4:
THE SCIENCE BEHIND PORN ADDICTION

I don't understand why I can't stop.

I've tried for fifteen years to quit porn. I hate it. It has destroyed every healthy relationship I've ever had. But I can never quit for more than a few days.

I tell myself every time it will be the last. But it never is.

Pornography is a demanding mistress. Unsatisfied, controlling, manipulative, she will enslave at all costs. Despair sets in when, after countless efforts to quit, pornography repeatedly reaches out her claws for her prey. Why is it so hard to break free?

In the last chapter we talked about some of the emotional reasons men turn to porn. In this chapter we're going to take a closer look at the addictive quality of pornography and why it is so difficult to quit. First, let's define "addiction."

> [Addiction is the] compulsive need for and use of a habit-forming substance (such as heroin, nicotine, or alcohol), characterized by tolerance and by well-defined physiological symptoms upon

withdrawal; broadly: persistent compulsive use of a substance known by the user to be harmful.[22]

Pornography is a harmful substance to the body, one which becomes compulsive and habit-forming in a short period of time. Truly an addictive substance, porn possesses both psychological and physiological control over your husband.

As real as an addiction to cocaine, pornography goes to places just as dark, and maintains just as strong a hold. This fact was cited in the 2004 U.S. Senate hearing on pornography's effects on the brain.[23] Pornography is recognized as a public health crisis in our nation and has become a subject of interest to our national leaders. Regulations and limitations are being publicly discussed. Yet the truth remains, porn addiction is different from a dependency on drugs in several ways, and therefore, more difficult to regulate.

Unlike drugs, porn is born of a God-given desire for something He created to be enjoyed: sex. It takes a beautiful gift from God and uses it for evil. In order for the government to make laws to address the damage

---

[22] *Merriam-Webster, s.v.* "Addiction." www.merriam-webster.com/dictionary/addiction (accessed September 24, 2018)

[23] Testimony of Dr. Jeffrey Satinover, M.S., M.D. to the U.S. Senate, Subcommittee on Science, Technology, and Space of the Committee on Commerce, Science, and Transportation. *Hearing on the Brain Science Behind Pornography Addictions and the Effects of Addiction on Families and Communities.* November 18, 2004. www.drjudithreisman.com/archives/Senate-Testimony-20041118.pdf

that has ensued from the porn industry, it would have to make rules based on morality, a topic most representatives tend to avoid in public arenas. A second way porn addiction is more difficult to address than an addiction to drugs is that you cannot separate the substance from the addict. You cannot simply remove the lustful mind from a person in the same way you can remove access to a drug. The mind is the drug.

A Chemical Reaction

Your husband continues to go back for porn due in part to a mechanism found on the molecular level. Quite simply, pornography has rewired your husband's brain. It has created chemical pathways which send his brain the message that he literally needs the images on his screen. This has occurred thanks to a neurotransmitter known as "dopamine."

Dopamine is a chemical in the brain that passes information from one neuron to the next. It is a messenger of sorts. It is infinitely complex in its functions and effects but in simple terms dopamine tells you something is pleasurable and it promises that repeating this same experience will be enjoyable. When dopamine is released, it communicates to your brain that whatever just caused the release is gratifying, and it motivates you to seek another release with the same action repeatedly. In a Reflexive Reaction, prolactin is released as dopamine wears off and creates the opposite effect; irritability, depression, the "low" after the "high." It tells you that you need another dose of "feel good" hormones, which encourages you to seek another dopamine release.

Dopamine creates reward pathways, signaling the brain to release other pleasure hormones in reaction to a particular experience. This process, referred to as "sensitization," makes it easier and faster to receive a flood of hormones in response to a certain substance. The more we turn to that substance for the pleasure reward, the deeper those pathways become. Like repeatedly hiking the same path through the woods, every pass beating the overgrowth down a little more until there is an easy trail to walk, the cycle of dopamine release quite literally carves new pathways that change the structure of your brain. This affects the entire body, including the nervous and immune systems. The chain reaction of dopamine and prolactin is the reason we feel irritable from not eating frequently enough and are driven to seek food. It is also why someone who is addicted to porn feels mentally and physically deprived without his "fix."

From exercise to eating to playing ball with your kids, dopamine is present. It is a natural part of God's design in many areas of life. The question is not, "How do I keep from having a dopamine release?" The question is, "During what activities do I want a dopamine release?" It's about intentionally deciding what you will receive pleasure from and actively managing your brain. It's about channeling the God-given chemical reaction and connecting it with God-honoring activities.

Dopamine is created by God. It's what drives us to pursue sex, food, and relationships with friends. The more deeply you enjoy a certain experience, the more often you will engage in that activity. We feel the pleasurable reward from a certain action, be it sexual release, a full tummy, or emotional satisfaction, and we seek to fulfill those cravings in the same way again and again. It's what helps us connect with our spouse through sex. We feel the overwhelming sense of pleasure sex produces in our bodies, and we seek the same source – our spouse – repeatedly to fulfill our sexual desires. Anticipation and expectation are part of that dopamine release and encourage us to eagerly engage in intimacy. That is how God created the physical relationship between a husband and wife. The problem comes when we seek the dopamine release caused by sexual gratification from sources outside of our marriage.

So what does this look like in relation to viewing pornography? A man views porn and dopamine is released, signaling that viewing this image is pleasurable. As the dopamine wears off, symptoms of withdrawal begin; mood swings, anxiety, fatigue, irritability, sleep disturbance, poor concentration. He is motivated by these feelings of deprivation to seek another release of euphoric hormones through the repeated action of viewing similar images. Each time he views pornography, the pathway deepens until there is a canyon-like gorge that must be flooded with dopamine or his body will feel withdrawal. The neuropathways in the brain of a porn addict are similar to those of crack addicts and alcoholics, and in the same way, keep him going back for more.

Michael Cusick described the process this way:

> Every time a person views porn, or eventually even thinks about porn, the burst of dopamine strengthens the connections between cells. The stronger the connection, the easier it becomes for cells to communicate on that path. This idea of the brain changing itself is called neuroplasticity. Whether learning to ski, learning to speak a foreign language, or looking at porn, the more we use a particular neuropathway, the more our brain changes, making the pathway stronger.[24]

The problem now comes with overstimulation of those pathways. Dopamine has been described as the "drug of desire" and the "gotta have it" molecule. It tells your brain to do whatever it takes to get a fix. However, overexposure to dopamine leads the brain to destroy dopamine receptors. The brain can only take so much of a good thing. Overstimulation is exhausting for the body. Even pleasurable messages can become too much to handle, so the brain starts to essentially shut down the system that reads those codes. So, when

---

[24] Cusick, Michael. "This Is Your Brain On Porn." The Counseling Moment.
https://www.thecounselingmoment.wordpress.com/tag/dopamine (accessed September 20, 2018).

someone says that watching R-rated sex scenes doesn't affect him, what he unknowingly means is that repeated exposure to such images has destroyed his God-given response to arousal. Overstimulation from scenes which once caused a dopamine release now renders him reactionless due to the destruction of receptors in his brain. This is what we call "desensitization." It's an overdose of dopamine. We no longer respond to the same level of substance, yet we're still left with a feeling of deprivation and drive to fill the void left after a rush. We continue to seek the next buzz.

Even though a guy no longer gets the same high from certain images, his brain feels the lack of dopamine and tells him to find it somewhere, and find it now. When this happens, porn users often go on dopamine binges, viewing hours upon hours of increasingly hardcore porn in search of a high. When even that no longer satisfies, they are left with two options: suffer the effects of withdrawal, or continue to seek a greater thrill. For many people, the effects of withdrawal seem unbearable. In addition, a lack of dopamine equals a lack of motivation for self-control. Thus, for many, escalation follows.

That's where it begins to get really scary. This is the stage where people begin to act out sexually. Dopamine is no longer kick-starting arousal, so they are driven to add another chemical reaction in hopes of stimulating a gratifying response.

Hello, adrenaline.

Adrenaline comes by stimulating emotions like shock or fear. It adds excitement to the mix. How do you get a rush of adrenaline when seeking illicit sexual satisfaction? By experimenting with ideas that once disgusted you. Viewing perversions such as homosexual acts or child pornography. Visiting strip clubs. Hiring a prostitute. Whatever will add shock value to get your heart pumping. Daring acts that initially appalled you bring a level of adrenaline that combines with just enough dopamine to create an explosion. Even the fear of getting caught can add enough excitement to the game to bring satisfaction. Now new pathways are created, causing a craving for these new escapades that once seemed revolting. The vicious cycle continues.

According to neurobiologist Peter Milner, our brains are attracted to that which is novel and unfamiliar. We seek variation. We get bored with the same old routine. We are beings that seek instant gratification, so when viewing soft-core porn no longer gives the same level of gratification we look for ways to spice it up. Normal sexual behavior begins to seem mundane and unfulfilling, even irritating. Not only does this cause a greater temptation toward perverse sexual behavior, but it leads to a lack of fulfillment in other areas of life as well. Depression sets in, and the lows can get extremely low. This is why porn addicts are often grumpy, lethargic, and sometimes suicidal. Nothing seems exciting anymore. They begin to become numb to the joys of life, and the only time they feel any pleasure at all is when they're engaged in escalating sexual fantasies.

For Christian men, the added guilt from the knowledge that their sin has separated them from God makes life bleak. They are ashamed of hurting their Savior but they feel a complete lack of control over their addiction. The temporary high from viewing pornography distracts from their misery, at least momentarily. When addiction rules, there is no room for the King. It should be no surprise that life lacks purpose.

Why doesn't this cycle of escalation happen with couples who are committed to purity in their marriages? Aren't they experiencing the same pleasure-reward pathways? Yes, they are, and it's what encourages them to return to their spouses when they seek sexual release. So why don't they get bored with their sex life? Why aren't their brains saying, "Okay, we need something more exciting, this just isn't cutting it anymore"?

There are several reasons. For one, sex with your spouse is not instant gratification. It takes effort and intentional exertion. God designed us to receive satisfaction from our efforts toward loving our spouse. Though fulfilling, this reward is by no means instantaneous, which makes it less addictive. Second, the dopamine reaction is reined in by the love we have for our spouse. Our physical relationship is not merely based on the high we receive but on the devoted love we have for each other. We do receive pleasure from a dopamine release during sex, but it's not the only reason we seek intimacy with our spouse. Other hormones, such as oxytocin, bind us to our spouses during physical and emotional bonding and this regulates the dopamine release. Instead of simply an act of selfish indulgence, marital sex is an expression of selfless love for our spouse. Sex is about more than just physical pleasure, so the brain doesn't get that same overload of dopamine. Men who keep their bodies (including their eyes) for their wives alone do not struggle as much with the temptation to raise the stakes. They are satisfied with their own cisterns (Proverbs 5:15-19).

Upping the Ante: Screen Addiction

We live in a digital age. Screens are everywhere. Work phones and computers are provided by companies. The school system uses digital devices to teach our students. We frequently turn to our screens to unwind or find a degree of emotional fulfillment through connections with people all over the world (who, we've come to believe, can communicate true friendship merely by clicking the "like" button). Screens, providing both easy access to information and an easy escape from real life, have become an integral part of daily life.

Ready access to technology is a mixed blessing. While we are able to obtain useful information like never before, screens in and of themselves pose a risk for addiction, making internet pornography more than just an appeal to sensuality. In days gone by, *Playboy* magazines and scantily clad poster women enticed men with visual pleasure. However, with the rise of digital access to pornography, the beast has emerged stronger than ever.

Screen addiction is a major problem in society today. How many of us have a compulsive urge to peruse our social media accounts, even if we just checked them thirty seconds ago? When you enter a restaurant, does the TV in the corner draw your gaze, making it difficult to focus on the table conversation? Colors flash. Lights glow. Even if the program holds no particular interest to you, still your eyes stray to the screen. You want to know what's going on over there, even if it's just a re-play from a sports game you care nothing about. The attraction of a constantly moving screen is one reason why children who struggle with ADHD are able to fo-cus for hours on a video game. It's not just that they're more interested in video games than in homework; it's that the screen is moving fast enough to please their quickly distracted brains.

Like pornography, an addiction to screens can ac-tually change the structure of the brain. It taps into that same pleasure-reward response and gives a dopamine release, creating pathways in the brain which demand a greater supply of the goods. The internet can take us anywhere we want to go, and our brains get used to go-ing there fast. We want more and more. This is one of the reasons internet pornography is particularly addic-tive. When you combine the compelling nature of por-nography with the mesmerizing effect of screen time, you wind up with a toxic formula.

Screens are a necessary part of most people's lives. A man immersed in the digital age is likely to struggle against two breeding beasts – porn addiction, and screen addiction. The two feed off of each other. This means that to break the one habit, he must recognize and fight both addictions. But how is this possible when we live in a world that revolves around screens?

After Joshua came clean about his porn use, we talked about how difficult it was to quit not only because of the quick access provided by screens, but because screens themselves had become a trigger for him. Joshua's access to pornography was almost 100% through the screens of his phone, our computer, and the movies we allowed in our home. Screens had become to Joshua what the sound of a bell was to Pavlov's dogs.

In Pavlov's famous study (circa 1889), he trained his dogs to come for their dinner every time he rang a bell. The dogs quickly learned food was coming when the bell rang. Eventually, all Pavlov had to do was ring the bell and the dogs would start salivating. They knew the bell meant access to food, and that thought triggered the physical reaction of drooling in anticipation. Similarly, every time Joshua used a screen, it stimulated a desire to access porn. In his physically altered brain, screens were associated with pornography so that each time he used a digital device it triggered temptation.

In order to stop salivating, Joshua had to remove the bell. To rewire his brain, he needed a complete fast from all screens. It wasn't enough just to tell himself that he wouldn't go there. It wasn't even enough to only use a computer if I was in the room. In order to make it possible to break his addiction to porn, we realized the screens had to go.

Part of what made this time different from all of Joshua's previous attempts to quit was that we removed digital temptation almost completely. We cut off data from Joshua's phone, stopped watching movies, quit playing video games, and severely limited internet usage to checking messages. We never had TV to begin with, but if we did we would have gotten rid of that, too. It was then we realized something surprising. Screens weren't just a trigger, and it wasn't only Joshua who had a problem. We discovered we had both developed an addiction to screens in and of themselves.

We both felt deprived in the beginning, and had a hard time adjusting to life without screens. We had gotten so used to zoning out in front of a movie every night that we didn't know what to do with ourselves anymore! I constantly fought the urge to scroll Facebook or stream Netflix. Even without viewing sinful content, the compulsion to stare at a screen combined with the impulse to see how much "approval" and "admiration" I could gain from a single post forced me to realize that breaking my own habit wasn't going to be easy. Our brains needed a reset.

We discovered for ourselves what researchers have been telling us for years. Screens are addictive, and the consequences are sobering. With heavy use of digital devices the rate of depression increases, health declines, and relationships suffer. This is so well understood by tech designers in Silicon Valley that many of them purposefully send their children to low-tech schools. Even top tech C.E.O.s such as Steve Jobs and Bill Gates have pointed out the danger of screens and enforced limits in their own homes. They recognized that the power of technology could negatively impact the emotional and physical well-being of their children.

This is vital to our discussion because a person's emotional welfare is a strong indication of his susceptibility to pornography addiction. When an addiction to technology results in isolation from healthy relationships, the risk for porn addiction rises dramatically. Technology fools us into thinking we are actively engaging with the world around us, when in reality we are quite isolated. We superficially network with people on our 'friends' lists without actually developing meaningful friendships, all the while ignoring the people right in front of us. Distraction, cursory glances, and shallow interactions define our day-to-day screen time and numb us to real life. This habit is prime fuel for an addiction. Connected to the internet and disconnected from the real world, it's easy to fall into the false sense of intimacy promised by digital porn stars.

When Joshua confessed his porn use we removed screens as much as possible for three solid months. Through happenstance, his confession came at a time when life got extra busy. We used to spend every evening watching a movie on Netflix, but life sped up with a cross-country move and more children being added to the family. We didn't have much time to waste on screens. Part of that was incidental, but part of it was purposeful, and it turned out to be one of the biggest factors in Joshua finally being able to quit porn. A lot of things changed all at once, and that made it easier to get rid of old habits. He was no longer tempted to log onto a porn site on the computer because he wasn't in the habit of using the computer at all. Once he was able to break his screen addiction, his porn addiction was easier to handle.

Screen addiction is a struggle more than most of us would care to admit. This, combined with the addictive nature of porn, makes for a bigger problem than anyone could have anticipated 30 years ago. In the days before digital porn, the enticement for men to look and lust was, of course, still there. But the added magnetization of screens makes internet porn an even greater temptation. In order to break the addiction to digital porn, it is wise to completely close the black hole of access through screens, at least for a time.

The Physical Price of Porn

Both pornography and screen addictions have harmful effects on a person's emotional and physical health. Both can lead to depression, irritability, low self-esteem, inability to empathize, loss of relationships, compulsive and impulsive behavior, and a propensity for alarming outlooks on life. Not only this, but porn also has an impact on a man's ability to be physically satisfied.

Judith Reisman observes that porn "castrates" men visually, training them to only be aroused by an image.[25] When a man has become addicted to porn, physical changes alter the brain to the point that God's design for sexual pleasure no longer satisfies. Many men complain of an inability to get an erection when attempting to have sex with their wives after viewing porn. Others admit that when having sex they can only reach climax if they think about the pornographic images they have seen. Impotence is becoming a problem even among young, otherwise healthy boys, as is apparent by the increasing number of teenagers showing up in doctors' office with complaints of erectile dysfunction. There is no medical problem with these boys. It's the porn.

When a porn addiction is present in marriage, it damages the physical relationship between a husband and wife, and inhibits their capability to connect on an emotional level during sex. Sometimes a man communicates, whether intentionally or unintentionally, to his wife that she is not enough of a woman to even arouse him, let alone satisfy him. Despite a loving husband's assurances that she is beautiful, a wife who cannot satisfy her husband's physical desires may feel unattractive and worthless in bed. Wounded by her husband's lack of sexual interest in her, she may suffer from a host of struggles of her own. Low self-esteem, obsession over her physical appearance, temptation to

---

[25] Reisman, Judith. "The Impotence Pandemic." Dr. Judith Reisman. www.drjudithreisman.com/archives/2007/10/the_impotence_p.html (accessed September 25, 2018).

win the attraction of a man who is not her husband. She may feel driven to sexual experimentation of her own to either figure out new ways of alluring her husband or to satisfy her own unmet physical needs.

If your husband is suffering from erectile dysfunction because of a porn addiction, do not blame yourself. That is a physical consequence of his own sin, not a reflection of your sexual performance. It is frustrating for both parties, especially when it is a problem in the early days of a husband's recovery from porn addiction. It can make him want to return to porn out of desperation to feel like a man again, and it can make you resent him even more. The bright side is that studies show most men suffering erectile dysfunction due to porn addiction return to their baseline function within just a few months of staying clean.

The Good News
We've talked about a lot of bad news in this chapter. Pornography has literally rewired the function of your husband's brain, and therefore his physical reactions. That's a huge load of information to digest. The good news is your husband's brain can change and be rewired again. Neuroplasticity means that not only can your husband's brain be wired for porn addiction, but it can be rewired for recovery.

Addiction does not override one's ability to choose. Just because your husband feels unable to control his sexual urges does not mean he doesn't have the power to stop the cycle of addiction. It takes 90 days for the brain to jump-start the healing process, and may take from six months to several years to return to normal, depending on the severity of the addiction. But it is possible, and he can do it. You can help him.

First, however, you need to help yourself.

Confessions of a Former Porn Addict

If I could have quit looking at pornography long enough to study why I felt compelled to look, I might have sought help sooner. But the science was against me. I was too hooked to care why.

If there was one thing I could convince every porn addict to do (or maybe even anyone having serious marital issues) it would be to turn off the screens. Seeing the difference in both Brittany and I when we went nearly screen-free was astounding. Even today I can see a negative difference in our family when any of us start using screens more than we should. I don't believe I would have ever stopped looking at pornography for more than a month if I didn't also stop using screens at the same time. Screens of all types can bring back or keep alive temptations that need to be slain. I had underestimated my enemy and mistaken his weapons as my friends.

Had I understood that it takes at least 90 days to begin breaking an addiction (had I even realized I was addicted in the first place), I might have had a better chance of permanently quitting the first time I tried. I wish I had known. I believe it would have offered me hope, and perhaps greater determination. 90 day is not a Magic Pill, but I wish I had known that I hadn't even begun to quit until I'd been porn-free for at least that long.

When I was viewing porn, I knew I was not thinking right, but I didn't know why or how to fix it. The *why* was my pornography addiction, and the *how to fix it* was to turn to God and leave the sin alone! I was so encouraged when I realized the good news that, in time, I could rewire my brain and think properly again.

CHAPTER 5:
THE TRAUMA OF BETRAYAL

Upon discovering your husband's porn addiction, it's natural to obsess over "Why?" That is a pivotal question, but one only your husband can answer. You may be able to help him figure out clues, but it is not a question you will ever be able to answer for him. So much of our mental energy as wives goes into trying to figure out and fix our husbands' problem. "How can I help him recover? How can I ensure he won't do this to me again?" It's easy to ignore our own need for healing when we're busy obsessing over how to make his addiction stop. It's harder to give attention to the more personal questions. "What about me? How am I supposed to react? Will I ever recover?"

Part of healing your relationship is seeking understanding. Seeing your husband's addiction from his side is an important part of recovering your marriage. While hopefully the previous chapters offer a deeper understanding of his struggle, it does little to address what *you* are personally experiencing.

There is so much more to your own healing than simply knowing why your husband looks at porn, or even hoping he can win the battle. It is when you shift the focus off of your husband and onto yourself and your own relationship with God that you begin to find freedom from pornography's clutch on your life.

Betrayal Trauma

"Don't come home," Marie texted Isaac. She had received an odd email that afternoon – an invitation to a chat room. Hoping it was spam, Marie decided to take a quick look at the search history on her husband's tablet, just to ease her mind. What she found made her head pound. Her world seemed to fall apart before her eyes as she scrolled page after page of sickening images. In their 10 years of marriage, Marie had never once entertained thoughts of infidelity. But now, as she browsed Isaac's bookmarked sites, she calculated the best way to show her husband what it felt like to be cheated on. Her own thought appalled her. And yet...

Does Marie's reaction surprise you? Probably not. Shock regularly brings to mind thoughts which would ordinarily be far out of character. Depression, rage, anxiety, a desire for revenge, and even suicidal thoughts are not uncommon reactions to a revelation of betrayal in marriage. Whatever your initial reaction to discovering your husband's porn use, I can assure you it was not unique. There is nothing you felt in that moment that has not been felt by hundreds of other women in similar situations.

It is normal to feel:

- Betrayed – You have been betrayed.
- Angry – Your husband has committed a sin against you and against God.
- Depressed – Your husband has destroyed your faith in your marriage.

- Overwhelmed – You're facing a crisis that will not suddenly disappear.

Feeling stressed, daunted, humiliated, and confused is to be expected as you process this crisis. Porn use is a violation of trust, and trust is one of the most basic foundations of your relationship. Take away trust, and the construct of your entire marriage starts to crumble. The cascade of emotions you are experiencing is a response to the disintegration of that trust. It's called "Betrayal Trauma."

As the smoke settles you find yourself standing in the rubble of what once was your marriage, wounded and scarred. It is indescribably painful. Your husband has broken his marriage vow to keep himself for you and you alone. He has given his eyes to other women and defiled what was rightfully yours. The discovery of this unfaithfulness in your spouse is traumatic.

The psychological term "Betrayal Trauma" occurs when someone in a primary relationship with us (such as a spouse, parent, or caregiver) violates our trust in a critical way. When this happens, your emotional and physical reactions can be just as intense as if you had witnessed a horrific car accident or survived a natural disaster. The psychological effects of betrayal trauma can sometimes even be classified as Post-Traumatic Stress Disorder (PTSD).

Traumatic events are followed by both emotional and physical shock. Some of the emotional effects of discovering your husband's porn addiction may include:

- Anxiety and Fear
- Hyper-vigilance (constantly on guard for another betrayal of trust)
- Feeling overwhelmed
- Withdrawal and Isolation
- Forgetfulness and difficulty concentrating on normal tasks
- Difficulty regulating intense emotions
- Avoidance (being unwilling to be around your husband or unable to go into public)
- Flashbacks (reliving the moment of revelation and mentally repeating the sequence of events)
- Negative thoughts (sometimes including self-harm and suicidal thoughts)
- Numbness and detachment

You may also exhibit physical effects of shock such as:

- Sleep and appetite disturbances
- Twitches and tremors
- Headaches
- Digestive complaints such as cramps, nausea, or stabbing pain
- Fatigue
- Body aches
- Dizziness

People who have been through betrayal trauma often feel as if they are going crazy; like reality is questionable, and everything about their relationship is a lie. They can't eat, they can't sleep, they obsessively replay events in their heads, and they can't focus on any one task. If you are experiencing these feelings after discovering your husband has been viewing pornography, you are not crazy. In fact, 70% of women who discover their husband's porn use suffer from symptoms of PTSD such as depression, anxiety, and insomnia.[26] The majority of these women suffer symptoms to such an extent that they interfere with their ability to function in important areas of life.

What you are experiencing are natural side-effects of broken trust in marriage. Learning how to work through these emotions takes time. Several months after Joshua confessed his porn use, I was speaking with an older woman in the church about how I just couldn't seem to get past the hurt. She told me that, statistically speaking, it takes a minimum of 36 months to really recover from a breach of trust in marriage. Three years. And I was surprised I was still struggling after only three months! Once I realized it was completely normal to still feel dazed and depressed, I was much more patient with myself in the healing process. It takes an enormous amount of time and effort to recover from broken trust, and it's not something that can be rushed to comply with a certain timetable. Some people don't feel able to completely trust even after three years.

---

[26] "Porn Stats." Covenant Eyes.
www.covenanteyes.com/resources/download-your-copy-of-the-pornography-statistics-pack/ (accessed October 2, 2018).

That's okay. There is no set timeline for recovery.

Betrayal Grief

In the wake of betrayal trauma, it is common to feel out of control of your emotions. You may experience severe mood swings and worry about your mental stability. A breach of trust leads to insecurity, and insecurity leads to feeling a loss of control over every area of life, including your emotional health. These reactions are partly due to grief.

Grief is a huge part of recovery from betrayal trauma. You are grieving over the fact that an essential part of your marriage has been lost. The trust a wife should have in her husband's faithfulness has suddenly been torn from you. You are likely to go through stages of healing akin to the stages of mourning the death of a loved one.

Just like mourning over death, the process of grieving loss of trust usually goes through five stages: Denial, Anger, Bargaining/Guilt, Depression, and Acceptance. Recognizing the emotional stage you're in helps you identify ways to cope and move toward healing. Keep in mind that these stages do not necessarily occur in this order, and you may find yourself back at square one as you repeat a stage you thought you had moved passed. Grief is not a clinical process; it looks slightly different for everyone. You may experience longer periods of one stage than you might expect, or even skip certain stages altogether. Generally, healing from betrayal trauma involves moving through each of these five stages at some point, though there are no rules for the grieving process. Give yourself compassion and grace. You are mourning the loss of a vital part of your marriage, but for most women these feelings do not last forever.

Denial

Wives often have an intuition that their husbands are being unfaithful in some way. When faced with evidence, though, sometimes it is hard to accept that this is actually occurring. Until your husband admits to his pornography use, you may try to find excuses for him, or try to think the best of the situation until you know all the facts.

Another side of the denial stage can occur when a husband has confessed porn use but his wife tries to minimize the impact, telling herself it's not really that big of a deal, or that "everybody does it anyway." This is not healthy for you or your husband. Pornography use is unfaithfulness, and is a very big deal spiritually, emotionally, and even physically. Do not minimize the hurt. Do not make excuses for your husband. He has wronged you and he has wronged the Lord. Denying the sinful nature of pornography will only lead to further heartache for you both.

During the stage of denial, life may become overwhelming or meaningless to you. Nothing makes sense. The shock is numbing and simply putting one foot in front of the other can be difficult. In these early days, you're just trying to survive. At first, you feel nothing, but as the reality of your husband's betrayal sets in, your emotions begin to let loose.

Anger

I never knew I was capable of such intense anger.

I'm in a near constant rage and I don't know why. I want to hurt him, but I want him to hold me.

Anger is usually the second response to a betrayal of trust in marriage. The intensity of the rage almost always comes as a surprise. Being so angry you could rip your husband's face to shreds with your fingernails, while at the same time wanting to run to him for comfort from the pain he has inflicted, can leave you in a state of confusion and guilt.

The stage of anger seems endless and can pop up even years after the incident occurred. Righteous indignation over the sin of pornography use is not wrong. "Be angry, and do not sin: do not let the sun go down on your wrath" (Ephesians 4:26). There are times when anger is justified. Even Jesus was angry over how people were wronging the Father and cheating others. Learning to differentiate between justifiable anger and uncontrolled rage, however, is important.

Anger over sin is not wrong. But too often the anger in this stage becomes irrational, aimed in the wrong direction. Your anger may not only be directed at your husband but also at yourself, friends, family, and even strangers. You may be angry with yourself for not seeing the signs of addiction sooner, with friends you blame for being bad influences, or with his parents for not raising him better.

All too often, we get stuck in the stage of anger. Anger gives one a sense of power, of regaining some control over a situation that is so desperately chaotic. Anger allows you to feel again. Suddenly, the numbness begins to subside and you find relief in the knowledge that you are capable of feeling, even if it is a raging fire. Anger is a natural part of grief. But learning to properly channel your anger is a necessary part of healing.

Bargaining or Guilt

In dealing with the impending death of a loved one, the stage of bargaining usually looks like attempts to make a deal with God. "If only You'll let this person live, I will devote the rest of my life to You." In betrayal trauma, this is the "What If?" stage. Your thoughts are constantly haunted by questions like, "What if I had taken better care of my physical appearance?" "What if I could turn back time and stop this from happening?" "What if I had never married this man?"

This is the stage where you may experience significant feelings of guilt and self-doubt over the role you played in your husband's addiction to porn. Questioning every tiny aspect of your marriage, you may obsessively examine your personal and marital history to try to pinpoint what exactly caused your husband to turn to pornography. Falsely placing blame on yourself for your husband's sins may lead you to bargain with yourself or with him (i.e. "If you will stay faithful to me, I will never say no to sex again.")

While there are always things we could do better in marriage, ultimately it is up to each individual to decide to walk righteously before God. You are not to blame for your husband's sins any more than he is to blame for yours. This is both a relieving and a depressing thought, because once you realize you are not to blame, you also realize you cannot keep this betrayal from happening again. Some wives would almost prefer to take the blame for their husband's porn use because they believe that if they could just change something about themselves, their husbands would remain faithful. This is not true. It is up to the individual to decide to live a holy life. You are not guilty for your husband's porn use.

Depression

As mentioned above, 70% of women experience some form of depression following a betrayal of trust in marriage. It's important to realize that this is a stage of grief and not a sign of mental illness. It is part of the process of coping, of coming to terms with the reality of your husband's infidelity. It does not mean that you will never experience joy in life again. That said, this is a scary stage for many women, and can cause some to contemplate self-harm or even suicide. Get professional help now if you are having thoughts of harming yourself.

1 Kings 19 gives an account of Elijah, a great man

of God, who struggled with a severe bout of depression. The wrath of Queen Jezebel was against Elijah and he fled into the wilderness. Exhausted and alone, he sat under a tree and prayed to God to take his life. But God was gentle with Elijah. First, the Lord allowed him to sleep. Then, He sent an angel to tell him to "arise and eat." God provided both food and water, and after Elijah took nourishment he lay down again to rest. A second time the angel came and told Elijah to arise and eat, which he did.

Then Elijah traveled to Horeb, the mountain of God. There he entered a cave and the Lord spoke to him, "What are you doing here, Elijah?" Elijah poured out his heart to God and told Him of the hardships he faced, complaining of how he was alone in serving the Lord. God did not chide Elijah. Instead, God told him to stand on the mountain, and the Lord Himself passed by.

In the midst of Elijah's deep depression and fear, God made His presence known. He encouraged Elijah with the promise that he was not alone; in fact, there were 7,000 people in Israel who still refused to bow to Baal. When Elijah was suffering from uncertainty, fear, anxiety, and exhaustion God gave him rest, food, water, assurance of His presence, and the confidence that he was not the only one serving Jehovah. Then, God gave Elijah a new mission and sent him back to work.

When we struggle with depression we need to be gentle with ourselves. Elijah's reasons for depression were valid. The Queen sought his life and it appeared he was the only one left who cared about serving the Lord. You, too, have legitimate reasons for feeling depressed. To not feel some sense of depression in the face of your husband's betrayal would be an unusual response. God knows your heart is broken, and He offers the same comfort to you as He did to Elijah. Take those gifts He provides and care for your own physical, mental, and spiritual needs.

Acceptance

The stage of acceptance does not mean you've come to a point where everything is totally okay. Most women will never feel "okay" with the fact that their husbands broke their trust. This stage isn't about acting like everything is fine, it is about accepting the reality of the situation and learning to live abundantly within the new construct of your marriage. Acceptance means you recognize that this is your husband's battle. While you can support him, you cannot fight for him. Embracing that concept gives you both freedom.

Your marriage has been scarred by a history of unfaithfulness. That is now a permanent brick in the unique structure of your relationship with your spouse. Accepting that fact means you are able to move forward, finding ways to work the broken pieces together to find resolution and rebuild trust. It means the new norm is for you to look out for ways to help your husband stay pure, and to be your husband's helpmeet rather than a constant reminder of the pain he caused you.

Acceptance is painful. We want to fix the past, undo all the mistakes and make it pretty and whole. That's not possible. Your view of the past has been forever altered with the knowledge of your husband's deceit and betrayal. Now you readjust. You now have a more accurate idea of the state of your marital history and you can move on to find ways of more openly addressing issues in your relationship. This more accurate view may not be pretty, but it's real, and that honest perspective is invaluable.

Acceptance does not mean your relationship with your husband has fully recovered; it means you recognize the damage that has been done, yet you allow yourself to see hope for the future. You are ready to live again, despite the pain. You invest in your relationship with your husband, and you face the struggle to restore your marriage head on.

Again, these stages of grief are not linear. You may jump back and forth between certain stages, or experience a few all at once. Whether you face these stages as outlined above or repeatedly return to a certain juncture, coming to terms with your husband's betrayal of your marriage vows necessitates a period of grief as part of the healing process. Give yourself permission to take as much time to grieve as you need.

Healthy Responses

Viktor Frankl, an Austrian psychiatrist and holocaust survivor, once wrote:

> Between stimulus and response there is a space. In that space is our power to choose our response. In our response lies our growth and our freedom.

You have no control over the fact that your husband viewed porn. You cannot control whether he looks at porn again in the future. The only control you have is over the way in which you respond. Not only in the face of the initial revelation, but also throughout the entire healing process. You will face situations which will test the limits of your own self-control. To a great extent, your response will determine the level of healing your marriage can experience.

How should you respond to your husband's porn addiction?

Pray Constantly

I believe the most important response you can give to this situation is prayer, illustrated well by the following story. Read how prayer helped rescue Tonya's marriage:

> I had dreaded this moment from the day we said 'I do.' I had never believed he would actually break free of the addiction. I kept a constant eye on the horizon and wondered just how long it would be before the storm broke loose. I didn't know when, but I knew it was coming.
>
> Because of that fear, I gave myself a degree of security by forming a plan. Back when Pete orig-

The Other Side of the Storm   103

inally confessed his history of pornography, even before our wedding, I decided how I would react if he ever gave into the temptation again. I knew that if I didn't react well in those first minutes, our marriage would be in serious trouble. Occasionally I would rehearse my plan of action. I envisioned it happening. I played out the scene in my head and determined that, even if Pete did start looking at porn again, I would be right before God in my response. It gave me strength to know that at the very least I had a plan that would help keep me from saying or doing things I would later regret. Like stabbing him in the eye with a knitting needle. That wouldn't be good. I had to have a better plan.

There came a day when Pete confessed he had been frequently viewing pornography since the beginning of our marriage. His words stung, but I could see that he was hurting, too. My heart ached for him. As hurt as I was, I wished I could take the pain of his sin away from him. It had cut him deeper than he could have ever imagined.

They tell you to make a plan in case of a natural disaster or national emergency. I had done just that in expectation of Pete's confession. When Pete told me everything, I did just what I'd planned. I silently left the room, and I fell to my knees in prayer.

That was it. That was all I had planned. It felt like déjà vu; like something so well-rehearsed it must have happened before. It was a little while before the reality of it all sank in. For the time being, I was merely going through the motions of a pre-laid course of action. When I had considered what my response should be, I knew I would need space to get my head straight, and I knew that the only One who could possibly hold us together in a moment like that was my Savior. I knew my first response had to be prayer.

I fell to my knees and wept bitterly, pouring my heart out to the Father for an hour and a half. I held nothing back. I admitted to Him everything I felt and everything I didn't understand.

When you learn that pornography has been a part of your husband's life, it is easy to turn inward and shut down. Opening up your bottle of emotions can be scary because it feels like once you let those emotions loose there will be no stopping the pain. Even prayer can seem like an agonizing risk. It is physically draining, and there is a temptation to run from the greatest Source of comfort, but it is imperative that you turn your feelings over to the One who cares for you most.

Tonya went on to say:

Pete and I both believe prayer was the most important thing that set the tone for how we dealt with the issue in the days to come. It was our first line of defense, and it continues to be our most powerful tool. I firmly believe that this was my first response only because I had decided years before how I would react if he ever confessed unfaithfulness.

Tonya's description of her soul-baring prayer reminds me of the cry of David's heart in Psalm 6:

Have mercy on me, O LORD, for I am weak; O LORD, heal me, for my bones are troubled. My soul also is greatly troubled; But You, O LORD—how long? Return, O LORD, deliver me! Oh, save me for Your mercies' sake! For in death there is no remembrance of You; In the grave who will give You thanks? I am weary with my groaning; All night I make my bed swim; I drench my couch with my tears. My eye wastes away because of grief (Psalm 6:2-7a).

This psalm speaks of the torment David's enemies have been to him. It is a prayer that God would rescue him from their hands and hold them back from their evil deeds against him. David's words are a vivid portrayal of the depth of anguish that is felt when the person closest to you betrays your trust. It is this very act of honest prayer that made it possible for both David and my friend Tonya to conquer the enemy of their souls.

Make prayer your first reaction. If possible, don't say another word to anyone until you have had some time to go to what Becky Blackmon refers to as "The Begging Place" where you can lay all your heart's hurt before God. Stay there as long as you need until you can be assured of God's strength and reaffirm that your highest priority is to please Him.

When you get off your knees, don't stop praying. Ephesians 6 tells us to put on the armor of God in order to face the wiles of the Devil:

> *Praying always with all prayer and suppli-*
> *cation in the Spirit, being watchful to this*
> *end with all perseverance and supplication*
> *for all the saints (Ephesians 6:18).*

As you go through your day trying to make sense of the devastation around you, keep your armor on. Make supplications for your husband and yourself. Ask God for wisdom to respond in a spirit of love and gentleness. Pray without ceasing (1 Thessalonians 5:17).

Is your soul greatly troubled? Do your very bones ache with grief? Then cry out to the Lord for His mercy. God wants to hear your heart. He wants you to lean on Him during this trial. He will provide the strength you need.

Give Grace

My own reaction to my husband's betrayal was not always as admirable as Tonya's. I was totally unprepared for how to handle the torrent of anger, bitterness, fear, and despair. It wasn't pretty. All at once I wanted to hold Joshua tight, forgive him, promise I would stand by him to the end, while at the same time I had a nearly overwhelming urge to punch him in the face. I was a pendulum of mixed emotions.

I have never been a violent person, but I had such a hard time refraining from hurling things at the wall. I wanted to break every dish in the house. But I had two little boys watching me intently. So instead I sat, hopeless, letting my mind numb itself to the realities of what all this meant.

Maybe you didn't handle the original discovery of your husband's porn use the way you wish you would have. Maybe you continue to respond in ways that frighten or concern you. Give yourself grace. You will feel emotions you may never have felt before. It doesn't mean you don't love your husband. It means you are human. You are not going to recover from this blow immediately. Take a few days off. Talk to a trusted counselor. Healing will take time, perhaps even years. Be patient with yourself.

Give your husband grace, too. He is broken, and he is hurting. His sin has devastated him as well. He needs your patience and he needs to know that you are with him. Though it is tempting to unleash all of your anger and hurl attacks, remember that he is wounded too.

Remember Jesus' words when the scribes and Pharisees brought to Him a woman caught in the very act of adultery? They wanted to know what Jesus would do with her, but instead His words put them to shame, "He who is without sin among you, let him throw a stone at her first" (John 8:7). We all stumble, but Christ is gentle with us. Give grace to your husband because God has given grace to you.

Communicate

It has been said that shock is God's anesthesia. Shock can ease the process of discovering details about your husband's porn use. Now, at the onset of the discovery of a porn addiction, is the best time to bring everything to light, before either of you have time to reconsider getting everything out in the open.

Though she initially told Isaac not to come home, Marie was able to calm down enough by that evening to allow her husband back into the house. They talked well into the night about everything Isaac had done, and by morning Marie felt much more peace. They were able to communicate with each other about the pain they were each experiencing. But there was one area where Marie remained uncomfortable. She expressed her concern about how her husband didn't want to share the details of his porn history.

> He says he just feels like it's over now and that hearing about it will only make me obsess more. I worry that I will cause unnecessary pain for both him and myself by asking him to explain certain things, but the questions continue to haunt me.

Isaac is not unusual in his hesitancy to give details. Most husbands want to protect their wives from the dark realities of their sin. Some women do not want to discuss specifics either. There is a school of thought that learning the details of your husband's porn use will only cause unneeded pain. However, in our experience, couples who are satisfied with leaving the details out of the discussion tend to have more difficulties later on. Women who do not know when or why porn use occurred find themselves increasingly more confused and insecure. Men who do not want to answer specific questions find themselves more easily falling back into pornography and deception. Failing to lay everything out in the light leaves temptations to breed in the shadows.

Open, honest communication is incredibly important from the very beginning, painful as it may be at the time. If you have questions, ask. Those questions will continue to haunt you until they have been answered. It's better to ask your husband upfront if you are wondering something specific rather than try to bury your concern. Often our imaginations are worse than reality, and it's healthier to face the truth – harsh as it may be – than try to silence the nagging thoughts.

Get as many facts as you are able to handle. It is your right to know exactly when and where your husband viewed porn. In the end your husband will probably be relieved to be able to tell you everything. Ask him when his pornography addiction began, what his triggers are, and how he accessed the material (computer, phone, books, etc.). Knowing the facts is important when it comes to creating a plan to beat the addiction.

Control Your Emotions

The three natural responses to threat are "Fight, Flight, or Freeze." The threat that betrayal has brought into your marriage will likely make you want to respond in one of those three ways. You may react out of fear and anger; yelling, fighting, and displaying your emotions very openly. That's the "Fight" instinct. You may be tempted to emotionally withdraw, or even physically leave. That's "Flight." Or, you may simply shut down completely. That's "Freeze." None of these reactions leaves much room for healthy communication.

These responses are self-preservation techniques. When you are ready to fight, flee, or freeze, take a step back and evaluate why you are feeling the urge to respond this way. Do your best to communicate those feelings to your husband without picking a fight or shutting down. If he only hears anger, he will not know your pain. If you completely withdraw, he will not see your heart.

Practice control over your responses so you can communicate in a way that is truly beneficial to your marriage. Be aware of your body's signals. If you begin to feel your muscles tighten, your heart race, or your head spin, that is a signal that you are likely getting ready to respond with Fight, Flight, or Freeze. Pull back. End the conversation and give yourself a break. Give yourself permission to feel, but not permission to give reign to every emotion.

Have Discretion

When the pain of your husband's betrayal is fresh, it is natural to shut down. As time goes on, however, it is also natural to feel a need to talk with someone. Professional counseling, both individually and as a couple, is extremely helpful in recovering from this kind of marriage crisis. However, it's not always possible to find or afford a licensed therapist. In those cases, it is wise to look for an older woman or a couple who can help you handle this issue in a biblical light.

It is good to find a mentor, but I want to caution against over-sharing your marriage problems. Family members often find it difficult not to hold a grudge. Your relationship with your mother may make her a wise choice for sharing your burden, or your mother may be someone who would be unable to let go of the pain your husband has caused her little girl. Your best friend might be someone you can count on to help you heal, or she may be someone who, due to past experiences of her own, can't handle the ugly side of your marriage. Be careful when choosing confidants. I am not going to tell you who you should or shouldn't share the details of your husband's addiction with, but be sure whoever you confide in is going to be a woman who:

- Will point you to God's Word for healing
- Will keep your confidence
- Will forgive and remain respectful toward your husband
- Will encourage you in your fight for your mar-

riage

We encourage being open about struggles. Telling your story benefits both you and others experiencing the same challenges as you share each other's burdens. However, being too free with particulars can be a risk to your marriage. The person you share intimate details of your marriage troubles with should be a carefully selected advisor. For everyone else, merely sharing that you and your husband are having difficulties and that you need the prayers of the church is sufficient. Specifying that the issue has to do with pornography is great. Just be careful not to be too open too early in the process of recovery. Protect your marriage from criticism and extra stress.

Forgive

We focus a lot on trust after betrayal, but that's not really the foundation of rebuilding marriage. Our first aim is to be able to forgive our husbands. Trust is necessary for completely restoring your relationship, but forgiveness… that is the critical first step.

There is a common misconception that forgiving someone means you must give them your trust. That is a false concept which can do serious damage to your marriage. Forgiveness does not equal trust. Just because you have forgiven your husband does not mean you necessarily trust him to remain faithful. In fact, premature trust can lead to increased temptations for him and greater insecurity for you. Your decision to forgive his sin against you doesn't negate the need for him to prove his trustworthiness.

Life is different now. Forgiveness doesn't mean pretending that everything is fine. You are not asked to simply forget everything your husband has done or act like he never cheated on you. You will remember. What does forgiveness look like, then?

Forgiveness looks like the cross.

We all at one time had a huge debt of sin we could never repay. God, through His Son, offers forgiveness for that debt. We don't deserve it, yet He freely gives.

How does He offer that forgiveness? We know He does not automatically forgive the whole world. Otherwise the whole world would be saved and there would be no need to teach others about Christ. God does offer forgiveness, but He offers it conditionally. A person must come to Him on His terms in order to receive His forgiveness.

> *If we confess our sins, He is faithful and*
> *just to forgive us our sins and to cleanse us*
> *from all unrighteousness (1 John 1:9).*

That word "if" is very important. It indicates a conditional statement. "If" we confess our sins, then He is faithful and just to forgive us. Forgiveness is dependent on confession, godly sorrow, and repentance.

> *Take heed to yourselves. If your brother*
> *sins against you, rebuke him; and if he re-*
> *pents, forgive him (Luke 17:3).*

There again, we see that little word "if." If your husband repents, then forgive. But for forgiveness to take place, repentance must occur.

God doesn't say you have to trust your husband; He says you have to forgive your husband in the same way God has forgiven you. We forgive because God has forgiven us (Luke 11:4). But we also realize that true forgiveness and reconciliation is dependent upon repentance. The Greek word for "forgive" in Luke 17:3 means "to send away; to let go; to give up; keep no longer." When we forgive our husbands for an addiction to pornography, it means we let it go. We no longer hold them accountable for that sin.

In the Old Testament, the Day of Atonement took place once a year. In Leviticus 16 we read of how Aaron was commanded to place his hands on the head of a scapegoat and confess the sins of the people. Then the scapegoat would be sent into the wilderness to perish (Leviticus 16:21). This is a picture of forgiveness. Aaron let the goat go. He sent it away. He didn't hang onto the sins of the people or constantly remind them of their wrongs.

In the same way, you must learn to let go of your husband's pornography use. Love "does not take into account a wrong suffered" (1 Corinthians 13:5 NASB). Don't hold your husband's past against him. Let go.

You can learn to forgive your husband because Christ forgave you. "How many times must I forgive my husband, Lord?" "I do not say to you, up to seven times, but up to seventy times seven" (Matthew 18:22). Do we not hurt God repeatedly by our sins? And yet He is always ready to forgive, opening His arms wide to embrace us and heal our self-inflicted wounds. He asks us to do the same with our husbands.

Trust cannot be rebuilt if you are not first willing to forgive. Once forgiveness has taken place, healing can begin. If you cannot let go of anger, bitterness, and resentment, you will never find reconciliation with your spouse. And that's what we're really after. Not just trust, but reconciliation – reuniting your marriage. To do that, you must first forgive.

Finding out your husband has been hiding an addiction to pornography is devastating. You feel beaten, shattered, and maybe even foolish for not seeing it sooner. Yet, forgiveness and restoration are possible. How you now choose to react can greatly influence your chances of recovering trust and reclaiming the marriage God wants for you.

> *Let all bitterness, wrath, anger, clamor,*
> *and evil speaking be put away from you,*
> *with all malice. And be kind to one another,*
> *tenderhearted, forgiving one another, even*
> *as God in Christ forgave you*
> *(Ephesians 4:31-32).*

Confessions of a Former Porn Addict

Immediately following my confession, I had a great need to convey to Brittany that she was my priority and that I wanted to be what she needed and deserved. I just didn't know how. I, too, was grieving over what I had destroyed, and I was scared I would never be the man she wanted. Those first few days were full of great concern for Brittany, and fear for how much I had damaged her. How much I had damaged *us*.

I remember wondering if Brittany would ever be able to get off the couch again. Would she smile again? Would she ever turn to me and see *me*, not what I had done? I knew she wouldn't leave me but I was so scared I would never really have *her* again. We would never be Brittany and Joshua again. And sometimes it felt like that was her fault, because she couldn't just "get over it." Couldn't she see all of that was in the past? The sin was gone, removed. I was ready to move on, act like this had never happened and get back to life as normal. (Though reflecting on it, I didn't want "back to normal." "Normal" was me looking at porn behind her back.) There were times when I was annoyed with Britt due to my own lack of understanding the consequences of my sin, but overall my greatest concern was how to fix what I had destroyed.

CHAPTER 6:
HEALING THE WOUND

Imagine you have a deep cut on your leg, and instead of cleaning and caring for the wound, you try to cover it up, pretend like it never happened. The blood pours, soaking through your clothes. It is obvious to everyone around you that something is wrong, but you don't talk about it; you hide your pain as best you can.

The wound gets infected. Still, you slap a bandage on and hope for the best. You take a little Vitamin C and tell yourself you'll be fine. The infection spreads. Now the poison is in your blood, flowing to the rest of your body. Yet you still refuse to acknowledge the problem. Eventually, what was once a raw but manageable wound becomes a life-threatening emergency.

A serious wound, without appropriate medical care, will fester until it destroys the body. So emotional trauma, without proper attention, has the potential to destroy the soul.

In the previous chapter we defined betrayal trauma and the inevitable grief that follows. Now let's focus on creating an environment conducive to healing from that trauma. Just as a physical wound needs care in order to heal properly, it takes intentional effort to heal your emotional wounds.

Focus on Your Own Healing
The best way to heal a wound on your leg is to fo-

cus on medicating your neighbor's infected arm, right? Of course not. But that's often how we approach recovering from betrayal in marriage. "If I can just fix my husband's addiction then my own emotional trauma will heal." Women often focus so wholeheartedly on their husband's recovery that they overlook their own needs. It's natural to want to jump right into helping your husband, but if you are not also working on your own healing, your marriage will never fully recover.

Part of personal recovery is to recognize that you cannot break your husband's addiction. No amount of filtering, questioning, prodding, or protecting will force him to change. Only he can do that; it is between him and God. You are responsible for supporting your husband, not fixing him. You have to get to a point where you are okay with letting your husband fight his own battle, loving him through it, while at the same time realizing that the only heart you can change is your own.

I love what Viktor Frankl once said. "When we are no longer able to change a situation, we are challenged to change ourselves." Every spouse is married to someone they can't control. You cannot manipulate this situation to bring about a certain result in your spouse. You can only affect change within your own sphere of control. Remember that, ultimately, self-work equals marital-work. Anything you do to improve your own emotional and spiritual health will positively impact your marriage. Let go of the fear of your husband failing and determine that, whether he stumbles or not, you will continue to work on your own relationship with God and your personal path to recovery.

If you have gangrene in your leg, you will be in no shape to help your neighbor get help for his infected arm. In the same way, when you do not focus on your own healing, your attempts at helping your husband recover are hampered. Support that comes from a place of anger, bitterness, or revenge is not beneficial to anyone. Acknowledge the barriers to your own emotional health and focus on getting to a place where you are whole again, regardless of your husband's choices.

Go to the Great Physician

What is the obvious first step when we are in a physical health crisis? We go to the doctor. This should be our first response when faced with spiritual calamity as well. Through the mercy of Christ's sacrifice, our own Heavenly Father happens to be our Great Physician, on call at all times. He is already caring for you.

> *The LORD is near to those who have a*
> *broken heart (Psalm 34:18).*

God is the Healer of your soul. The critical first step to healing from your husband's porn addiction is to deeply connect with the Physician. Healing does not come from being assured that your husband will never betray you again. It comes from finding true peace in Christ. When you seek Him with your whole heart you will find Him (Jeremiah 29:13), but if you do not turn to the Physician you will never experience the wholeness that comes from His faithfulness.

When Joshua's porn addiction came to light, I was suddenly thrown into a spiritual crisis. I realized how much I had relied on my husband for my own spiritual security. I had set him on a pedestal and, yes, I still loved the Lord and still studied His Word, but when my hero fell I felt stranded spiritually. I felt so distant from God. I needed to first fix my relationship with Him before my marriage could begin to heal.

Any time you are faced with marital strife it points to a bigger issue; a spiritual conflict in either your life or your husband's—or most often, both. Where there is marital discord, there is spiritual warfare.

> *For we do not wrestle against flesh and*
> *blood, but against principalities, against*
> *powers, against the rulers of the darkness*
> *of this age, against spiritual hosts of wick-*
> *edness in the heavenly places*
> *(Ephesians 6:12).*

In the case of a porn addiction, there is an obvious spiritual fracture in your husband's life. This has the potential to either create or magnify a crisis in your own heart.

Paradoxically, rather than encouraging us to run to the Great Physician, betrayal can leave us doubting the love of the Father and the authenticity of His people. It is quite normal for a betrayed woman to suspect every man she knows, eyeing them with distrust. Every time a guy pulls out his phone she thinks, "Mmm hmm, I know what he's doing." She may begin to imagine all kinds of scenarios about the men in her life. This can lead her to doubt the spiritual leaders of the church, or hesitate to go to them for counseling, thinking she can't trust them because they are surely hiding some awful sexual sin, too.

A crisis of this kind can also cause a woman to question everything she thought she knew about God. "If I thought my husband loved me and he was capable of such betrayal, can God's love be genuine? Does He even care about my heartache?" The beauty of trauma that leads to a trial of faith is that these questions can actually strengthen your walk with God. When we take these questions to the Physician, begging His help as we navigate our doubts, we allow Him the opportunity to prove His faithful love. This in turn strengthens our dependence on Him as we observe firsthand His healing power.

The only cure to the pain you are going through is to go to the Great Physician. What if, when faced with a physical health crisis, you turned away from the only specialist who knew how to save your life? It would be an unfathomable, foolish decision. It is even more foolish to withdraw from God when He seeks to soothe your pain and carry you through this trial. If you do not bring your heartache to Him and immerse yourself in His Word you sacrifice the one relationship that is able to provide you with complete peace and healing.

Clean the Wound

Before a wound can begin to heal it must first be

cleaned. You must remove all the grime, dirt, and debris before it creates an infection. If it is a serious injury, you will need help with this painful process.

Betrayal trauma is a serious injury. It requires assistance from others in order to fully understand and address the pain. Find your support network and allow them to help you heal. Ideally, this will include friends, mentors, support groups, and professional counseling. Groups such as "Sexaholics Anonymous" have chapters which provide support to wives of addicts. You can also find online resources and support forums. Taking part in discussions with other women who are in similar situations can give you tools and perspectives you might not otherwise consider.

While you can find ways of coping on your own, you will greatly benefit from seeking professional help. Couples counseling is extremely beneficial for addressing the difficulties in your marriage, while individual counseling gives you the opportunity to concentrate on the personal challenges of your healing journey. Both are advisable. A counselor familiar with porn addiction will understand the specific challenges you experience and will help you explore deeper emotional issues.

Your response to your husband's betrayal involves a lot more than just a reaction to what he has done. It is rooted in several other issues you might not even realize are there. How you react has a lot to do with your own history, the makeup of your personality, the needs of your love language, the way you saw your family respond to negative situations in childhood, and any trauma you may have experienced in previous relationships. A good counselor can help you articulate your emotions, identify what is triggering your reactions, explore your personal history, and create a personal game plan to work toward healing.

The cost of professional counseling often deters couples from seeking assistance. Don't let that keep you from getting the help your marriage needs. The value of your marriage is much higher than any cost counseling might incur. Having someone to talk with in person who is familiar with betrayal trauma is a huge blessing. However, if professional counseling is not an option for you, at least talk with someone you trust to provide sound wisdom.

One of the biggest assets to healing from your husband's betrayal of trust is to have an objective person help bear your burden (Galatians 6:2). God gave us other Christians to help get us through some of life's darkest times. Lean on your Christian family. Reach out to a mentor. Allow others to help clean your wounds.

Address Underlying Issues

An underlying health issue can prevent a wound from healing properly. If your body is already compromised by a disease such as diabetes or leukemia you are not going to recover from an injury as quickly as someone without a pre-existing condition. If you experienced emotional trauma prior to your husband's porn addiction, your reaction to his confession may be rooted in, or at least compounded by, unresolved turmoil.

Joshua has been clean for over six years now. Do I consider our marriage to have "recovered"? Yes, I do. Do I still have emotional trauma I am working through as a result of his betrayal? Absolutely, and in some ways I believe I always will. That's not to say he is completely to blame him for the challenges I continue to face. To a large degree, I still struggle because of my own history with relationships. Some of the issues I have to work through aren't really because of his betrayal so much as triggered by his betrayal. I brought emotional baggage into our relationship just like he did. Many of the struggles I face in our relationship in regard to his porn use are really just symptoms of a greater struggle in my own spiritual life.

How much of your turmoil is a direct result of your husband's betrayal, and how much of it is trauma that was already present and is merely being triggered by his disloyalty? For instance, if you previously experienced betrayal of some kind, the betrayal you are now facing is going to be that much more staggering, that much more horrific.

Your ability to heal has a lot to do with identifying past, unresolved trauma and recognizing how this plays into your current marriage crisis. For me, it was the issue of protection. When Joshua and I started courting I had just come out of an abusive relationship in which I was left vulnerable and unprotected. Joshua stepped onto the scene at the exact time I needed out of a relationship that was damaging my health, my spiritual life, and my mental stability.

Cue the dramatic music and enter Super Joshua.

I don't mean to be totally flippant. I truly believe it was God's Providence that brought my husband into my life at the exact time I needed his strength. But when two years later I discovered he had been lying to me, going behind my back, and breaking our wedding vows, I remember thinking, "Wait a minute. This is the guy who was supposed to protect me. Why wasn't he protecting me from himself?" The still-tender wounds I had from that previous relationship were suddenly reopened. Trauma upon trauma that was already there.

We all have history that affects who we are today. We operate based on past experiences. When faced with a crisis such as porn addiction in marriage, it's important to be honest about the way those past experiences are influencing your path to healing. This is one reason I so highly recommend counseling. It helps you dig up the past and connect it with the present, while giving practical steps to use in the future.

What might be influencing the way you react to your husband's betrayal? A family member who was addicted to porn in your childhood? A different kind of addiction that destroyed relationships you held dear? Take time to identify and address any underlying emotional turmoil so you can give yourself the best chance at complete healing in your marriage.

Supplement Your Healing

I'm sitting at Table65, a chic café bistro on Main Street. I'm taking myself out for the first time in my life. It's kind of a surreal experience, sitting here sipping on a chai tea latte, wondering why I've never done this before. I'm loving it. After a long week with cranky toddlers and a series of unsuccessful attempts at conquering Mt. LaundryMore, I needed to find some sanity. There is a gentle rain outside and only one other person in the dining area. Soothing music is playing softly in the background, and the only other sound is the whirring of the cappuccino machine. It's delightful.

And yet, I feel guilty.

I know I'm not unique in this feeling of self-contempt even while I am attempting self-care. It comes from years of being told that "me time" is selfish, that good mothers always put their children first. "Sorry, Mama, you gave up the right to a moment of silence the day you welcomed that darling babe into the world." Now there are children to bathe, the husband to feed, a budget to balance. How can a woman justify taking time away from her responsibilities to do something purely for herself when there is so much to do for others?

Then there is the swing in the opposite direction, a push (mostly by marketers trying to sell you on expensive products) to indulge yourself because "you deserve this." I am a sinful creature who truly deserves nothing good the Lord has ever done for me. God did not create me to pursue every whim of my flesh. But that doesn't mean God wants me to be harsh to my body or ignore my needs.

While it's true there is nothing I could ever do to deserve God's love, God has chosen to love me enough to send His own Son to die for me. If God thinks I am worth that much, what right do I have to tell myself that I am not worthy of self-care? What right do I have to neglect my needs and deplete my own energies so that I have nothing left to use in service to my King?

Self-care isn't about deserving a fifteen minute break, or an extra nap. It's about recognizing that if we do not care for ourselves physically, emotionally, and spiritually we will not serve God to the best of our ability. Self-care is something we do out of necessity so we can properly tend to the tasks God has set before us. The confusion comes when we mistake self-indulgence for self-care. There is a difference between engaging in an activity for its healing benefits and simply using it as an escape from pain. Losing yourself in hours of mind-numbing TV shows or eating an entire box of donuts is not self-care; that is escapism. Rather than running from pain, the goal of self-care is to fortify your heart and mind so that you are able to face your pain and use it to grow.

It's hard for women in general (and mothers in particular) to allow themselves to care for their own needs. We are nurturers by nature. Everyone else comes first. Outside pressures from the world say you've never done enough and you never are enough until you are drop dead exhausted from sunrise to sunset. It's hard to find time to take care of the basics, like brushing your own teeth. When it comes to taking care of an unseen need such as mental health, self-care is usually on the "optional" list, right there under "teach the preschooler the Greek alphabet." It just never happens.

Listen. When it comes to recovering from your husband's porn addiction, self-care is not optional. The adage is true: You can't help someone else put on their oxygen mask until you have first secured your own. During this time of rebuilding trust in your marriage, self-care must be a top priority.

When recovering from a wound or illness, it's important to support your body with supplements and healthy routines. It is the same when recovering from emotional wounds. Stress is extremely hard on the body. When cortisol levels rise, you are susceptible to increased blood pressure, stomach aches, chest pain, insomnia, constipation or diarrhea, muscle cramps, and general malaise. Do your best to listen to your body's cues and give it the proper nurture it needs. If you don't, you will find it increasingly difficult to handle the emotional stress you face over the coming months.

Physical Self-Care

- **Drink plenty of water.** Under normal circumstances you need half of your body's weight in ounces of water. If you weigh 180 lbs, you need to drink 90 oz of water daily. Under stress, the body becomes dehydrated more quickly, so you need to increase your daily water intake.

- **Eat as well as possible.** Going through the shock of discovering your husband's porn addiction may put eating well at the bottom of your list of worries. It's easiest to grab whatever is available or, worse yet, not bother to eat at all. Without fuel for your body, your emotions are more difficult to regulate. Reach out to your support network. When people offer to do anything they can, they mean it. Take them up on their offer of support and let them know that meals would be a fantastic way to help you through this season.

- **Care for your body.** Exercise is excellent for mental health. Turn on some positive, upbeat music and go for a walk, or join the local ladies gym. Keeping your body fit not only gives you a physical outlet for stress, but also helps keep you from spiraling into depression. At a time when it can be difficult to crawl out of bed, do your best to care for your physical body. Shower, dress, put your make-up on. Maintain your regular routine as much as possible.

- **Rest.** Times of stress mean your body needs plenty of sleep. It's common for insomnia to plague women facing betrayal trauma, but do your best to get the rest you need. Limit screen time, listen to relaxing music, take a bath. Do whatever it takes to help your body release tension. You may find you need a nap during the day. This extra sleep can be beneficial as long as you are not sleeping too much as an escape from reality. Get as much rest as you can, whether that is actual sleep or simply stepping back from some unnecessary activities for a while.

- **Let some things go.** Don't worry about keeping the house up to your usual standard. If people are fed, clean clothes are available (they don't have to be folded or put away), and the trash is taken out occasionally, you're doing great. You are recovering from a major trauma. This is not the time to feel guilty about a sink full of dishes.

Mental Self-Care

- **Give yourself space.** You need a little bit of time to yourself each day. Take 15 minutes to meditate on a Psalm each morning. Sit outside. Breathe in the crisp morning air. Do something that involves you, by yourself, focusing your thoughts every morning on the important things in life. Keep a thankfulness journal or practice calming breathing techniques. Give yourself time every day where the only thing you have to do is be still.

- **Try something new**. Do something fun outside the house at least once a week. Take an art class. Learn an instrument. Plant a garden. Eat at a new restaurant. Get involved in a volunteer position. Find something that inspires you, focuses on the beauty in the world, and gives you something to think about other than the problems in your marriage. Your mind needs that breather. Consider how you want to feel (energized, creative, accomplished, rested, healthy, connected, challenged, peaceful, etc.), then choose activities that help give you that feeling.

- **Laugh**. Whenever possible, find the humor around you. Allow yourself to smile in spite of the heartache. Laughter truly is one of the best medicines, even for a broken heart. Giggle with your children, watch a funny movie, read newspaper comics. Laughter releases healing endorphins which ease tension all over your body. It may seem impossible at the moment, but make it a goal to find something to laugh at every day.

- **Practice relational care.** Grab coffee with a friend. Call a family member. Meet new mom friends at the park. Do something that connects you with other people and forces you outside yourself. Just as pornography isolates the user, so betrayal trauma isolates a spouse. The less connected you are to loved ones, the harder it will be to recover emotionally. Positive friendships remind you that healthy emotional connections are still possible. This doesn't take the place of your connection with your husband; it simply reminds you how to connect in safe, healthy, nonthreatening ways.

- **Seek connection with your husband**. Don't shut your husband out. Emotional connection helps build back trust. At this stage it is more important than ever to develop a daily habit of reconnection with your spouse; just five minutes a day to sit and talk. As soon as you are able, begin a weekly date night. At first these dates may be full of emotional conversation, but slowly you will find that they become enjoyable again. Allow your husband to woo you, and encourage any effort he makes to fan the flame of romance in your marriage.

- **Allow space for grief**. It's been said that the only cure for grief is to grieve. There is no way to heal from trauma except to face the trauma. It is going to be a painful journey. There is no skipping that part. Allow yourself plenty of time every day to grieve. Cry, pray, journal. During this period of grief ask for and accept help with meals, chores, the children, and anything else you need. Emotional self-care means honestly assessing your stage of grief and allowing yourself the time you need to process without rushing.

The Story of a Scar

Behind every scar there is a story.

The smooth, slightly discolored spots on my knee are a permanent reminder of the time I fell while roller skating when I was seven years old. The memory of my babysitter removing the deeply imbedded gravel still makes me cringe. I have a scar on my side where the handle of my bicycle once dug into my ribs when I did a flip going down a steep hill. My least favorite scar is the perfectly round pock mark right in the middle of my forehead, evidence of my bout of chickenpox at age four. Oh, how my brothers loved to tease me about that one!

Deep wounds leave lasting scars. The more serious the injury, the more visible the scar. We can become embarrassed by these marks, eager to hide the imperfections under clothes and make-up. Or we can allow our scars to tell a story.

Your husband's betrayal will leave a lasting mark. While you can heal and find greater satisfaction in your marriage than you ever thought possible, you will never forget what he has done. Just as a healed wound leaves behind a scar, the memory of this period will remain. But scars are more than just reminders of pain, aren't they? They are a testimony of survival, evidence of healing. The memory of pain dulls over time, leaving room to celebrate the victory.

God created our bodies with an amazing ability to recover from injuries. Layer upon layer, your body builds back tissue until the wound is closed. Though the skin looks different now, the injury is repaired. He created us with similar emotional resilience. We will be changed by our experiences with trauma. We might act and even look different, but given the chance our hearts can heal. God can take the broken pieces of your life and mold them into unfathomable beauty.

> *Therefore, if anyone is in Christ, he is a*
> *new creation; old things have passed away;*
> *behold, all things have become new*
> *(2 Corinthians 5:17).*

Will you allow the Great Physician to bind your soul back together? Or will you constantly pick at the scabs and reopen the wound? If you allow yourself the time and conditions to heal, your emotional scars can be used to God's glory as you share your story of recovery with others. The wounds that bleed today can one day become a testimony of survival and a witness to God's powerful healing. What story will your scars tell?

Confessions of a Former Porn Addict

I was terrible at recognizing Brittany's need for self-care. She needed to take a step back to put things in perspective, but I saw her withdrawal as a threat to us. Her silence scared me, but it was her way of coping. She needed lots of quiet time and would invite me in as she was ready. Once I understood her need for mental space, I was better able to support her.

One of my biggest problems with Britt's silence was that I didn't understand that healing was her goal. I felt threatened by anything that I didn't see as a resumption of normal, or a focused act at bringing us closer. I found change frightening. But change was a good thing. There had to be a new normal. Brittany let me know what she needed so I could better understand how to be there for her, and she assured me that our marriage was her priority, second to God. That made me willing to do anything it took to help her with her own self-care.

Chapter 7:
What Winning Looks Like

In Proverbs 6, King Solomon warns against dealings with harlots. In verse 27, he cautions, "Can a man take fire to his bosom, and his clothes not be burned?" Messing with the harlots in the porn arena is playing with fire. Partaking in the passing pleasure of viewing their bodies brings consequences. Your husband has taken fire to his bosom, and in the process has burned your heart as well. There is healing, but recovery from this sin takes long-term commitment and dedication to pleasing God above all else.

You wonder if you will ever be able to trust your husband again. He's probably wondering if he will ever be able to trust himself. Thankfully, regaining purity of mind is possible. It takes years of hard work, but the brain, with its wonderful neuroplasticity, is capable of being reset and rewired to abhor what is evil and find pleasure in what is godly.

Here's the reality: *You are not in control of whether your husband beats porn*. The importance of this truth cannot be overstated, yet it is one of the hardest parts about this whole situation to accept. You must release control and trust God to bring healing to your husband, and your marriage. You are your husband's cheerleader; but winning a victory over porn is your husband's responsibility alone.

Does that mean there is nothing you can do? Just

sit back and *hope* he's staying faithful? No! There are things you can do to encourage your husband, and, to some degree, hold him accountable. But you will never force him to change. Your encouragement is only as helpful as he allows it to be. If he wants to be pure, he will gladly accept your assistance, but if not, then nothing you say or do will make him stay clean.

You will never be able to filter everything your husband sees. At some point you have to let go of your fear and trust your husband to guard his own heart. That is a scary thing for a wife of an addict. If you can't control everything he sees and everywhere he goes, how can you be assured that he's truly changed? You cannot read his heart (only God can) but there are outward indications that your husband is truly ridding his life of porn. If your husband is serious about quitting pornography, you will catch glimpses of radical change in his life. When you see these changes, allow them to restore seeds of trust in your marriage.

What Does Winning Look Like?
Characteristics of a Man of Godly Sorrow:

1. His heart is pierced by his sin.
2. He avoids places of temptation.
3. He is completely honest.
4. He humbly takes responsibility.
5. He is willing to do whatever it takes to build trust.

Characteristics of a Man of Worldly Sorrow:

1. He minimizes his sin.
2. He continues to frequent places of temptation.
3. He is defensive.
4. He arrogantly blames others.
5. He is unwilling to do what it takes to break free from sin.

He Will Realize the Seriousness of His Own Sin

If your husband is serious about breaking his addiction to porn, he will realize the seriousness of his sin. He will not excuse his lust as a "typical male pastime." Lustful sensuality is sin against God and against you, his wife. It separates him from the Father and makes it impossible to have right relationships in any area of his life. The wages of sin is death (Romans 6:23), and as long as this sin continues without repentance, the consequence is eternal damnation. Lewdness is a work of the flesh, and those who practice such things will not inherit the Kingdom of God (Galatians 5:19-21).

Your husband must admit he has a genuine addiction and understand that he has been a slave to pornography. Someone once said, "Pornography cannot be overcome until the pain exceeds the pleasure." Once your husband realizes the stronghold pornography has on his life, he will accept that serious steps must be taken to reach freedom. In order to get to that point, he must first recognize that pornography controls him. His thoughts, his actions, his life have been dedicated to serving sin. Until he reaches that point, he won't be able to seriously address the recovery process.

> *For observe this very thing, that you sor-*
> *rowed in a godly manner: What diligence it*
> *produced in you, what clearing of your-*
> *selves, what indignation, what fear, what*
> *vehement desire, what zeal, what vindica-*
> *tion! In all things you proved yourselves to*
> *be clear in this matter (2 Corinthians 7:11).*

Knowledge of his sin should lead your husband to godly sorrow and produce true repentance, a change of life. A man who is truly repentant will show obvious fruits of repentance in his life. It's one thing for a man to be sorry for what he has done. It's another for him to repent in a manner that changes his course and leads him to stand pure before God. It's easy to be sorry for sin while still making excuses for the darkness in one's heart. Repentance leads to humility and acceptance that no one else is to blame for the sin he has committed. When your husband has this attitude of true repentance, it will be clear to you.

A man who is humbled by his sin will cry out to God with the psalmist:

> *O LORD, You have searched me and*
> *known me. You know my sitting down and*
> *my rising up; You understand my thought*
> *afar off. You comprehend my path and my*
> *lying down and are acquainted with all my*
> *ways. For there is not a word on my*

*tongue, but behold, O LORD, You know it
altogether...Search me, O God, and know
my heart. Try me, and know my anxieties;
and see if there is any wicked way in me,
and lead me in the way everlasting
(Psalm 139:1-4, 23-24).*

He Will Prepare For Spiritual Battle

*Beloved, I beg you as sojourners and pil-
grims, abstain from fleshly lusts **which war
against the soul**, having your conduct honorable among the Gentiles, that when they
speak against you as evildoers, they may,
by your good works which they observe,
glorify God in the day of visitation
(1 Peter 2:11-12, emphasis mine).*

A man who is serious about beating porn will prepare for battle. Once your husband has acknowledged
the seriousness of his sin, he will prepare himself spiritually to wage war against lust. He will study the Word
and meditate on the path of God which leads away from
sin. Many men stuck in pornography avoid reading the
Bible because they know it will condemn them. While
the Bible does condemn sin, it's also the only place to
learn how to be freed from bondage to sin. Those in sin
are dead; they lose their spiritual life. To gain victory,
your husband must allow Christ to renew his life
through the Word, taking him from being dead *in* sin to
being dead *to* sin.

*Likewise you also, reckon yourselves to be
dead indeed to sin, but alive to God in
Christ Jesus our Lord. Therefore **do not let
sin reign** in your mortal body, that you
should obey it in its lusts. And do not present your members as instruments of unrighteousness to sin, **but present yourselves
to God** as being alive from the dead, and
your members **as instruments of righteousness to God** (Romans 6:11-13,
emphasis mine).*

*Let us walk properly, as in the day, not in
revelry and drunkenness, **not in lewdness
and lust**, not in strife and envy
(Romans 13:13, emphasis mine).*

*Therefore put to death your members which
are on the earth: fornication, uncleanness,
passion, evil desire, and covetousness,
which is idolatry (Colossians 3:5).*

He must recommit himself to God, understanding
that he is not his own (1 Corinthians 6:19), and that he
must not be mastered by anything but Jesus (1 Corinthians 6:12). Christ must be his Lord, not sin. He must
put on the whole armor of God in order to withstand the
wiles of the Devil (Ephesians 6:10-17). The strength of
the Lord and the power of His might will enable him to
fight the battle against lust.

As he grows in the Lord through this journey, he

will keep a careful watch over himself and pray that he does not fall into temptation (Matthew 26:41). He draws near to God, cleansing his hands and purifying his heart before the Father (James 4:8). He recognizes that this is a battle, not only for his own soul, but also the souls of those around him. When your husband is preparing himself for spiritual war, you will see it, if you pay attention.

He Will Address Infections of the Heart

Last summer, our two-year-old was bitten by a tick and contracted Lyme disease. While we treated the main infection, we later learned that co-infections are frequently transmitted along with the Lyme bacteria. These co-infections caused a myriad of problems in our little guy, which seemed unrelated. Anxiety, hyperactivity, eczema. We tried to address each symptom individually, but we weren't able to clear them up until we realized they were all caused by a second strain of bacteria transmitted along with the Lyme.

Like Lyme disease, pornography addiction often comes with several "co-infections" of the heart. A man who is addicted to porn will often also struggle with unrealistic sexual demands and expectations of his wife, compulsive lying, outbursts of anger, masturbation, and a desire for isolation. The porn addiction has side effects that must also be recognized and addressed as part of the recovery.

Lying

Human beings have always been a self-deceiving

lot. Eve convinced herself it was the serpent's fault that she sinned. She should have stopped herself at the first glance at the forbidden fruit. It was her choice, her action—but she told herself otherwise. But she didn't stop with self-deception; she then tried to convince God Himself that it wasn't her fault!

One sin leads to another. Your husband may convince himself of many lies when he is using porn. Things like, "It doesn't hurt anyone." Or, "Looking is not the same as touching." Or, "It's natural; everybody does it." When you convince yourself of a lie, it's much easier to convince others.

Wives have often told me that their husband's *lying* about his porn use destroyed their security more than the fact that he viewed it in the first place. Marriages are killed by distrust. When a wife can't trust her husband to be honest, she will struggle to trust him to stay faithful.

Just as Adam and Eve tried to cover up their sin by clothing and hiding themselves (Genesis 3:7-8), porn-addicted men will go to great lengths to keep their sin in the shadows. They put a great deal of thought and effort into covering their tracks. The stress of keeping this sin a secret leads to frustration, anger, self-loathing, depression, and a web of deceit which can do more damage than the porn use itself. When your husband is serious about quitting porn, he will pursue openness and honesty in everything connected to this sin.

Sinful Attitudes

Another co-infection of porn is a twisted view of relationships with women. It damages the emotional side of marriage, leading husbands to become cold, disrespectful, and unable to be empathetic to their wives. He may seem distant, irritable, or even cruel at times, because pornography use physically alters the reward center of the brain and shuts down your husband's ability to emotionally connect with you.

His satisfaction with your physical relationship goes down as well, and eventually the only way he can find sexual fulfillment is by seeking increasingly hardcore porn. He will find himself insatiable for sin, "having eyes full of adultery and that cannot cease from sin" (2 Peter 2:14). What he sees on the porn stage, he comes to expect in his physical relationship with you. When you can't give him the results he wants (because porn is fake and there is no way you can mimic what is portrayed there), he becomes frustrated and scornful.

This is partly a deflection of the disgust he feels for himself. The guilt, self-loathing, and frustration he feels is unbearable. In an attempt at self-preservation, he rejects those feelings and flips them around, looking for someone to blame. It is a defense mechanism to keep those who love him at arm's length, never letting anyone know the real source of his pain. When your husband begins to free himself from pornography, you will notice a softening of his heart and attitudes.

Masturbation

Masturbation is a huge part of most porn addictions. It is commonly accepted, even among Christians, that masturbation is a natural part of being a guy, and that the actual act of masturbation is not wrong. It is sometimes even recommended as a way to avoid pornography (which doesn't work for most men, by the way). As Mark McWhorter points out in his article "Body and Sexual Development in Children and Adolescents",

> "To state that masturbation is necessary and useful to overcome sexual sin is to assume there is no other way of escape... [M]any of those who masturbate state it is for personal pleasure or expediency. There is no intent of refusing a sexual pleasure. There is no intent on using the sex organ for a God ordained purpose. There is no mortification. Instead there is a giving in to temptation."[27]

The Bible does not explicitly talk about masturbation. However, masturbation violates several principles of a God-honoring marriage. God designed sexual desire to be fulfilled between a married man and woman. Masturbation is self-gratification and involves only one party. "The wife does not have authority over her own body, but the husband does. And likewise the husband does not have authority over his own body, but the wife

---

[27] "Body and Sexual Development in Children and Adolescents" by Mark McWhorter

does" (1 Corinthians 7:4). Sexual gratification is a gift husbands and wives give each other. Your spouse is the only one who can legitimately satisfy your sexual needs. To give yourself a cheap alternative is to defraud your spouse of the honor of being the sole fulfillment of your sexual desires. When masturbation is used as a way of escape from stress, boredom, or loneliness it is an abuse of the gift of sexuality in marriage.

"The overwhelming majority of males engage in fantasizing while masturbating, and few share these fantasies with romantic partners."[28] There is almost never a time when one masturbates solely to thoughts of his or her spouse. When a man does think of his wife, it usually involves situations she has never actually participated in. In essence, he is creating sexual stimulation from a make-believe woman he merely calls his wife to ease his conscience, similar to how a woman might wrongly daydream about a fictional version of her husband who is more suave, tender, or emotionally attentive.

Often, men involved in pornography will masturbate while watching porn, leading to a vicious cycle of masturbating to memories of that porn, then seeking even more porn to masturbate to, then more memories, etc. For a recovering porn addict, the chance of masturbating without fantasizing about previously viewed

---

[28] Psychology Today, "Male Sexual Fantasies and Masturbation" https://www.psychologytoday.com/us/blog/sex-life-the-american-male/201401/male-sexual-fantasies-and-masturbation

porn is slim. The pleasure he is able to give himself only serves to stimulate a desire to seek sexual activities apart from his wife.

Masturbation is addictive, and often leads to an inability to be stimulated by one's spouse. Like porn, masturbation can lead to erectile dysfunction due to the neurochemicals released during the act. When a man is used to pleasing himself, he finds it more difficult to be aroused and properly stimulated by his wife. It is difficult for him to be pleased during sex unless he fantasizes—just as he does during masturbation. When pornography is beaten, masturbation is easier to conquer.

Leading into Sin

A fourth common co-infection of pornography is leading one's wife into sin. A man who is addicted to porn may encourage his wife to watch with him, reasoning with her that as long as they are doing it together, there can be nothing wrong.

Bringing pornography into marriage together is just as wrong as using it independently. Encouraging sexual stimulation from something and someone other than one's spouse is a defilement of the marriage bed, whether it is done together or separate. I know wives who hesitated to stand up to their husbands on this issue because they felt it would be unsubmissive. Honoring your husband does not mean partaking of his sins! You are responsible for your own soul and must not allow him to lead you into sin.

It may take time for him to recognize they are

problems, but a man who is serious about breaking his porn addiction will strive to overcome all areas of weakness. You will know your husband is winning when he doesn't see porn as an isolated issue, but as a symptom of a heart infected with compounding sins.

He will do Whatever It Takes to Free Himself

It's easy to say you will do anything to break an addiction, but it's harder to follow through. It's a much bigger deal than saying you don't want to be involved with that sin anymore. Steps must be taken and boundaries set to keep temptation at bay.

Many have pointed out that pornography thrives in part because of its Accessibility (anywhere at any time), Affordability (usually free), and Anonymity (can be viewed anonymously). It isn't possible to completely alter these aspects of porn, but there are steps that can be taken by your husband to make it much more difficult to view. Some measures will be drastic, but they are worth his soul. When you see him taking these steps, be encouraged.

He Will Bring It All to the Light

The surest way for your husband to denounce his sin and get the help he needs is for him to bring his struggle to the light. Going forward and asking for the prayers of the church may seem mortifying to both you and him, but our brothers and sisters cannot help if they do not know our struggles. Scripture encourages us to confess our sins to one another.

> *Confess your trespasses to one another,*
> *and pray for one another, that you may be*
> *healed. The effective, fervent prayer of a*
> *righteous man avails much (James 5:16).*

Sin thrives in secrecy, but the Light kills corruption. This heart of humility, coming to the church for help, displays the very attitude required to defeat porn.

> *He who covers his sins will not prosper,*
> *But whoever confesses and forsakes them*
> *will have mercy (Proverbs 28:13).*

Aside from going forward for prayers, your husband needs to be completely transparent with you. He needs to bring it all out in the open and hold nothing back. Not every church member needs to know the details of his sin, but he must be completely honest with you, of all people. When he is willing to reveal all, he is winning.

He Will Learn To Possess His Own Body

A man must learn where to put his eyes. Matthew 5:27-30 discusses the severe nature of lust, calling it adultery of the heart. A large part of refraining from lust is averting one's eyes from what is sexually enticing. Job's covenant in Job 31:1 should become a mantra in your home:

> *I have made a covenant with my eyes; why*
> *then should I look upon a young woman?*

Your husband must learn how to control his bodily

cravings, and keep from acting on the temptation to view pornography and indulge in masturbation. He must learn to master every part of his body, bringing his thoughts into captivity in obedience to Christ (2 Corinthians 10:5). It is the will of God that we all learn how to master our own bodies to honor the Lord.

For this is the will of God, your sanctification: that you should abstain from sexual immorality; that each of you should know how to possess his own vessel in sanctification and honor, not in passion of lust, like the Gentiles who do not know God (1 Thessalonians 4:3-5).

When your husband practices control over his body, he is winning.

He Will Avoid Places of Temptation

It's true that our society is saturated in sexual sin. It's hard to avoid graphic depictions in America today. Corinth was a similar culture, rife with sexual perversions. Certain places were worse than others. Corinth had a plethora of pagan temples, many of which were equipped with temple prostitutes for the pleasure of the so-called worshippers who would frequent them. The saying "When in Rome do as the Romans" is often used to excuse frequenting places of pervasive sin (often sexual sin). Instead, we should be teaching our churches, "When in Corinth, avoid the temples!"

Your recovering husband must avoid places that

are particularly prone to glorifying lasciviousness. This includes running around with friends who are loose in their morals, attending sports events where cheerleaders dance provocatively, going to a populated beach or swimming area. This may even mean he needs to change jobs if his company sends him on business trips alone with female co-workers, or if he finds that his time in hotel rooms is too much of a temptation. He must do whatever it takes to avoid places of temptation. When he takes drastic steps to avoid temptation, he is winning.

He Will Flee Temptation

When King David found himself on the roof gazing at Bathsheba as she bathed, he should have immediately left the place of temptation. When your husband finds himself in a place where he is tempted toward sexual sin, he needs to get off the roof!

Genesis 39:12 says that when Potiphar's wife caught hold of Joseph's garment and commanded that he lay with her, he left his garment in her hand and "fled and ran." He was so intent on removing himself from this dangerous situation as quickly as possible that he left his clothes behind!

1 Corinthians 6:18 warns us to "flee sexual immorality." 2 Timothy 2:22 directs us to "flee also youthful lusts." The word "flee" in these passages means to "seek safety by flight," to "shun or avoid something abhorrent," and to "escape safely out of danger."

Sometimes a man finds himself in a situation he

did not anticipate. Whether put there by his own choice or by the choices of others, he must flee to safety, removing himself completely from the dangerous situation. Encourage your husband's efforts to flee sexual sin, even if it means abandoning an event you are enjoying—because when he does, he is winning.

He Will Turn His Heart

> *And because lawlessness will abound, the*
> *love of many will grow cold*
> *(Matthew 24:12).*

When a man is addicted to pornography, eventually his love for God and his love for his wife grows cold. He begins to forget about God's sacrifice to bring him out of his sins. He starts to view his wife as merely an object for sexual gratification or, worse yet, something standing in the way of his sexual pleasure.

In overcoming a porn addiction, your husband will learn to turn his heart first to God. When he looks to God to satisfy his soul, the appeal of pornography will lessen. He will then turn his heart to you, his wife. When your husband puts the Lord first and you second, you will know he is winning. He will remember to think of your needs and desires first, and he will look to you for sexual fulfillment. He will heed the wisdom of Proverbs 5:15-20:

> *Drink water from your own cistern, and*
> *running water from your own well. Should*
> *your fountains be dispersed abroad,*

streams of water in the streets? Let them be
only your own, and not for strangers with
you. Let your fountain be blessed, and re-
joice with the wife of your youth. As a lov-
ing deer and a graceful doe, let her breasts
satisfy you at all times; and always be en-
raptured with her love. For why should
you, my son, be enraptured by an immoral
woman, and be embraced in the arms of a
seductress?

God Delivers

At times, it seems like an impossible battle, but your husband can beat pornography one day at a time. When he's initially coming out of porn addiction he might feel desperate, helpless, and hopeless. A change of outlook will help him see that the obstacles to purity can be overcome. Encourage your husband to remember Philippians 4:8-9,

Whatever things are true, whatever things
are noble, whatever things are just, what-
ever things are pure, whatever things are
lovely, whatever things are of good report,
if there is any virtue and if there is anything
praiseworthy—meditate on these things.
The things which you learned and received
and heard and saw in me, these do, and the
God of peace will be with you.

Kevin Majeres, on his website purityispossible .com, recommends three mindsets for breaking the cycle of porn addiction.

1. See challenges as opportunities (rather than threats) for growth.
2. Stay deliberate and mindful during periods of lustful cravings.
3. See each trial as practice which will strengthen you for greater challenges.

These mindsets can serve as guards for your husband's heart. Ultimately, though, freedom is only possible in Christ.

> *For the grace of God that brings salvation*
> *has appeared to all men, teaching us that,*
> *denying ungodliness and worldly lusts, we*
> *should live soberly, righteously, and godly*
> *in the present age (Titus 2:11-12).*

It is Christ who delivers and makes salvation available for all men. Your husband cannot do this on his own, but through Christ he can have victory. "I can do all things through Christ who strengthens me" (Philippians 4:13).

It is God who provides the way of escape.

> *No temptation has overtaken you except*
> *such as is common to man; but God is*
> *faithful, who will not allow you to be*
> *tempted beyond what you are able, but with*
> *the temptation will also make the way of*
> *escape, that you may be able to bear it*
> *(1 Corinthians 10:13).*

You will know your husband is ridding his life of porn when you see him walking worthy of the call of Christ (Ephesians 4:1). He will pray, adjust his thinking, and strive towards being a living imitation of Jesus. He will remember that there is One who stands in the gap for him.

> *Seeing then that we have a great High*
> *Priest who has passed through the heavens,*
> *Jesus the Son of God, let us hold fast our*
> *confession. For we do not have a High*
> *Priest who cannot sympathize with our*
> *weaknesses, but was in all points tempted*
> *as we are, yet without sin. Let us therefore*
> *come boldly to the throne of grace, that we*
> *may obtain mercy and find grace to help in*
> *time of need. (Hebrews 4:14-16).*

God knew all along the struggle of your husband's heart. The Lord knows how intense the temptation is because Christ Himself was tempted in every way as we are. Yet He is sinless, and He knows how to help your husband refrain from sin. Jesus sympathizes with your husband's weakness. It is before His throne of grace that your husband can find mercy and help for his fight against pornography. He just needs to turn to the One who knows every detail about his history, the One who knows how to help your man overcome his past. This same God loves your husband with an everlasting love, and is giving His all to draw him back into His arms.

> *The LORD has appeared of old to me, say-ing: "Yes, I have loved you with an ever-lasting love; Therefore with lovingkindness I have drawn you" (Jeremiah 31:3).*

The most joyous moments of your marriage will come when you see your husband fully relying on Christ for forgiveness, strength, and deliverance. It is then that you can have confidence that he is fighting pornography – and winning.

Confessions of a Former Porn Addict

I regretted my sin of pornography from the very start. I didn't have to *learn* to be ashamed of what I had done. What I had to learn was the difference be-tween shame and godly sorrow with genuine humility in repentance. Shame and humility are often conflated, but they are very different attitudes.

I was remorseful. I really wanted it to end, but I failed to choose a different course. I wanted a different outcome; I wanted to stop looking at porn, but I didn't change paths—so it should have been no surprise when I kept ending up at the same destination. I couldn't see how to change directions. Partly because I did not want to do what needed to be done. I bought into the stupid lie that I should not need to pray about my struggles or seek help from others. I didn't think God should have to help me. I had gotten myself into this mess and I should be able to quit by myself. Can we say, "Satan's Lies 101"? It was a worldly sorrow, a combination of shame and pride.

Part of my aversion to praying was that the more I prayed about it, asked for forgiveness, asked not to be led into temptation, and asked for strength to resist temptation, the guiltier I felt when I fell back into sin. It was as though trying harder just made me more hypo-critical. Sometimes I would pray in earnest, and some-times I would pray knowing I was insincere. There were times I would pray, "Lead me not into temptation," knowing full well that I wanted the temptation—and longed to give into it. Almost like (but not nearly as purely as) the man who cried out to Jesus, "I believe, help Thou my unbelief," I wanted Christ to somehow take away my desire for sin. But God doesn't force righteousness on us. We are given the choice to choose Him and His way.

When I decided to get out of pornography for real, I quickly realized I had no idea how to fight a spiritual battle. I wanted to put up a good fight against Satan, but I was at an absolute loss as to how that is done. As I learned what was necessary to battle, I realized my old ways were still alive, and strongly encouraging me to not bother with ridiculous things, like an accounta-bility partner, accountability software, and a whole host of other things. They were not perfect safeguards, and could not completely keep me from pornography, so they seemed like pointless irritations. I had no ap-preciation for the fact that I was in an all-out war.

Once I started to understand this long-term war mentality, I think Brittany finally began to see some change in me. Not that it was a 'lightning from the sky' sort of thing. In truth it was gradual (and I'm certain it was frustratingly slow for her). When I finally repented with godly sorrow, I was willing to do whatever it took to win the war.

One of the things I found essential to my battle plan was to make sin inconvenient. Not impossible (because sin is always possible), but less convenient. Being humble about my sin made me willing to do even the "ridiculous," like calling some guy once a week and talking about how I was doing. Yes, I could lie to him (and he wouldn't have known the difference), but that would be an intentional choice to head back toward sin. Having to call this guy was a defense and, as I learned, a valuable one. I finally realized it didn't matter how pointless something seemed; if it helped even a little bit, it was worth the inconvenience.

Another thing I found necessary was complete honesty in all areas. I once bought Brittany an anniversary card at Wal-Mart while I was picking up other items for her. The total seemed a little higher than it should have been, and we went over the receipt together. I rattled off everything I bought, except for the card. Keeping this purchase from her began to eat at me so much that I had to go back and tell her. I cannot ever be anything but open, especially with Brittany. Because lying has previously been a struggle for me, even this level of secrecy was too close to allowing Satan a foothold. I know that no matter how strong I may be, the enemy will try to use my weaknesses to pull me back into sin. Therefore, I've got to be excessively above board as a preventative measure.

Even though safeguards don't guarantee victory, having defenses that weaken your enemy's attacks are well worth the trouble. Landmines are not placed in hopes that they will win the war, but in an effort to slow the enemy's advance. I needed to understand that while nothing would *win* the war but a complete commitment to God, I could make the battle much easier with a lot of small weapons, tools, and defenses to help me hang on.

CHAPTER 8: SUPPORTING YOUR HUSBAND

"I'm not going to babysit him. I can't stress about every little thing he sees."

As my phone conversation with Rachel continued, she relayed the challenges she and James had faced in recent weeks. She had discovered that her husband of six years was back to porn after swearing his addiction was over. The lust that had ruled his life in their early days of marriage raged once more. Rachel was furious. She insisted they get counseling immediately, and James agreed. Despairing, Rachel told the therapist, "He says he's sorry and that he wants to quit. I love him and I want our marriage to work, but I just don't know what to do. He keeps saying he needs me to help him stay clean, but I'm not the one who can make that decision."

Probing a little, the counselor asked James what kind of help he was looking for from Rachel. "I've told her some of the shows she likes me to watch with her make it very difficult to keep my mind where it needs to be. I've asked that we quit watching those, but she just gets mad." In addition, James shared that they were subscribed to several magazines, including one which Rachel particularly enjoyed for the fashion tips but which often featured provocative women on the front cover. Every month when these magazines arrived in the mail, James found himself warring against lust.

Rachel admitted she knew some of the shows they watched had questionable aspects, but she thought they should be mature enough not to let those present a temptation. When her counselor suggested she help James conquer his lust by removing things that triggered temptation, Rachel was indignant. "It's up to him to not look. Everyone keeps saying this isn't my responsibility, and they're right. If he wants to look at porn, I can't stop him. Why should I give up something I enjoy 'just in case' he doesn't control himself? I trust that from now on he will refrain from lusting after a stupid, airbrushed magazine model! If he's so changed, he'll prove it."

Rachel's words revealed some of her own heart issues which needed to be addressed before her marriage could heal. She needed to recognize that the filth she was enjoying was just as ungodly for her to view as it was for her husband. While she may not have understood the danger these shows posed to her own purity, they certainly didn't depict what was good, lovely, pure, or noble. If they had, James probably would not have found them tempting. Rather, they depicted ungodly relationships, glorified unrighteousness, and glamorized licentiousness. These were not just triggers for her husband's porn addiction. These were things which Rachel herself had no right to view. Apart from trying to help her husband overcome porn, Rachel needed to see that ungodliness has no place in any

Christian's life. "I will set nothing wicked before my eyes; I hate the work of those who fall away; it shall not cling to me" (Psalm 101:3).

Hopefully one day Rachel will be able to trust James not to lust after magazine pictures and TV characters. But let's not confuse Rachel's approach with actual trust. She did not trust her husband to refrain from looking at inappropriate images. That's why they were in counseling. What she was doing was testing her husband's determination to remain clean by refusing to do anything to clean up the atmosphere of their home. She wanted James to rebuild her trust by proving that, even when surrounded by filth, he would not stumble. So she left stumbling blocks around the house.

That is not love!

It was interesting to hear Rachel complain that James did not love her because he looked at porn, while at the same time defending her actions of tempting him to sin. Instead of lovingly helping James in his battle, Rachel was putting stumbling blocks in her husband's path to purity.

> *Then He said to the disciples, "It is impossible that no offenses should come, but woe to him through whom they do come! It would be better for him if a millstone were hung around his neck, and he were thrown into the sea, than that he should offend one of these little ones" (Luke 17:1-2).*

Your husband faces enough visual offenses in the world. Woe to you if you knowingly allow offenses to bombard him at home!

While Rachel's attitude is understandable, expecting James to suddenly snap out of his addiction and simply not look is foolish. A porn addiction does not go away overnight, nor does it end without deliberate action. Regaining purity of mind is an uphill battle. Why make it harder? Leaving temptation lying around your home and expecting your recovering husband not to look is like expecting an alcoholic to live in a bar and not drink. It is not a wife's fault if her husband struggles with porn, but it is her own sin if she tempts him in order to ascertain the level of his commitment.

You cannot change your husband, but you sure can encourage him. Rather than sit back and wait for James to prove himself, Rachel should have taken an active role in helping her husband regain purity. A wife can't keep her husband from sin; however, there are things she can do to help him overcome his addiction. A man has to be willing to do whatever it takes to reach victory over lust. A wife should be just as willing to do whatever it takes to help get him there. Work *with* your husband, not *against* him.

Help Your Husband: Communicate

Discussions about purity and protecting your relationship are not a one-time deal. Though often uncomfortable, these conversations should continue throughout your relationship. The more you discuss your mutual struggles, the easier it will be to secure the walls around your marriage.

It takes a great deal of courage for your husband to admit to you that something causes him to struggle. This confession of weakness is contrary to the world's idea of manhood. It can be hard for him to talk about because he would like to think he's not really affected; that he's above temptation. He may also be hesitant to discuss his triggers with you if they are things you really enjoy, like a particular location or a favorite TV series. Perhaps he feels something shouldn't bother him and he feels guilty that it awakens his desires.

Talking about the details of a struggle with sin is awkward and embarrassing for most people. It's especially hard for men to talk to their wives about areas where they have a hard time keeping their minds pure, because they despise continually causing pain. The Devil loves to play on your man's desire to protect you. Satan wants your husband to keep his struggles to himself because a man struggling alone is much easier to entice.

Communication is crucial to keeping temptation at bay. You can encourage your husband in this by making it as easy as possible for him to tell you when and how he's having a hard time. Encourage him to open up by asking specific questions about his fight. Many couples have shared that it is helpful for the wife to ask the husband on a daily basis how he is handling temptation about pornography. Knowing he will have to look his wife in the eye every day and answer whether he has stayed clean is a huge motivator to keep his eyes from evil.

As difficult as it may be, keep your reactions in check; do your best to avoid shaming your husband when he admits he's struggling. Just because he is *tempted* to look at porn does not mean he *has* looked at porn. Though it is painful to hear your husband is having a hard time staying pure, remember that temptation does not equal sin. Listen to his heart, offer encouragement, and help him come up with ideas to maintain purity.

When your husband communicates that he needs to avoid certain places or get rid of certain movies, show your appreciation. Rachel was frustrated that James couldn't handle things she thought he should be able to, but she would have done better to appreciate that he was communicating his needs. If your husband has told you the mall is a place he needs to avoid, don't ask him to go with you "just this once." If he's told you he's not going to the theater anymore because of all of the racy previews, don't ask him to make an exception for a movie you've really wanted to see. Value the fact that he has been honest enough to tell you what causes him a problem, and respect him enough to do everything in your power to help him avoid threatening places.

Communication goes both ways. You need to know where your husband is in his fight with porn, and he also needs to know how you're doing in your journey toward healing. Always say what you are thinking. Say it nicely, but say it honestly. Do not say things for the sake of revenge, but do honestly let him know what you are feeling and how you are handling the knowledge of his betrayal. Something like, "I'm struggling to understand what makes you want to look at that stuff," goes much further toward repairing your relationship than spewing venomous words for the sake of inflicting pain.

Letting your husband know when you struggle to trust him helps him realize he needs to make a greater effort to assure you of his faithfulness. This in turn helps him keep a closer guard over his own heart. Communicating during times when you trust him more helps encourage him to keep fighting for purity. When he knows his woman is cheering for him, he's more motivated to prove his integrity. He doesn't want to let you down. Honest communication cultivates intimacy, and intimacy is one of the greatest ways to help your husband stay pure.

Help Your Husband: Cultivate Intimacy

Intimacy following betrayal may be the last thing on your mind. When we are wounded, the natural response is to withdraw. We avoid the source of pain in an effort to protect ourselves. While this may soothe the hurt for a time, it will ultimately cause the wounds in your marriage to fester. Intimacy, a close connection with your spouse, is a God-given wall of protection for both you and your husband.

Intimacy is more than just sex. Intimacy is a bond that draws two people together in a unified relationship with common goals and desires. It is more than physical contact; it is also friendship and emotional connection. It comes from flirting, playing together, sharing dreams, showing each other respect and joining your hearts together through prayer and study of Scripture. Aside from his relationship with God, it is this intimacy with you that will go the furthest in helping your husband remain pure.

We are beings created to crave intimacy. God Himself desires closeness with His children (James 4:8). He also knows we humans desire a close connection with other humans. He provided the wonderful relationship between husband and wife to fulfill those desires for deep intimacy. It is both a gift of pleasure and protection which keeps us strongly bonded to our spouses. When intimacy is missing from marriage, a void is left which we have a strong desire to fill—and Satan gives us plenty of suggestions on how to fill it.

Intimacy is important, not only because it helps your husband stay focused on you as his one and only, but because without intimacy you miss so much of what God intended for your marriage. God didn't design us to simply live as business partners, but to be friends, lovers, co-laborers in the Kingdom. Withdraw from the intimacy God wants for your marriage, and you cheat yourself out of the blessings He has in store for you through your husband.

The idea of a close relationship with the man who destroyed your trust is scary, and perhaps even repulsive, yet this is exactly the time when it is most important to draw near to him. Satan would love nothing more than to widen the chasm in your relationship. He knows that few things have as great a potential to destroy souls as destroying a marriage. Every effort you make toward intimacy with your spouse is a blow against Satan.

Start slow. Unrealistic expectations for the level of intimacy after betrayal will only cause stress. You are, in effect, building trust from scratch. Think about how you developed a close relationship with your husband when you were dating. Just as it took time to trust your heart to him then, it will take time to restore your trust in him now.

Little efforts go a long way. Start by setting aside time every day to reconnect. Leaving minutes at the end of the day for just the two of you to fill each other in on the day's events is a non-threatening way to strengthen your marriage. This isn't a time to delve into deep issues. You're not forcing emotional closeness. You are just sharing how your day went. This is a time to practice the pleasantries of friendship.

Along with daily reconnection, set aside a weekly date night. Did the words "date night" make you cringe? Is it more than you're ready for? This is not your typical romantic evening out. At least, not at first. The idea is to give you space to discuss your relationship at a specified time. This is especially important if you have children. With little ones, it's difficult to find time to talk about serious matters. Their little ears do not need to hear your strife. Leave them with a babysitter and take time away for just you and your spouse to focus on your marriage. Whether you stay home to talk, go out to dinner, or take a walk in the park, this weekly time is important. It may not feel much like a date at first, but you may be surprised at how it leaves room for romance to blossom naturally.

As you are able, work time into your schedule to enjoy life together. Rediscover each other's interests, take a class together, play games, study the Word and pray together. Your marriage needs these chances to rekindle the spark of love and companionship. Remember that porn preys on those in isolation. Engaging your husband in his hobbies and discovering new interests together helps strengthen the bond between you, making loneliness and boredom less of a risk. Above all, seek every opportunity to grow together spiritually, and to seek the Father in all things as you restore and renew the love you have for one another.

Knowing one another on a deep emotional level is an important part of marriage. When the emotional connection is reestablished, it is easier to rebuild the romance and physical intimacy that seemed threatening and unthinkable in the beginning. Even then, it can be daunting.

It's fine (and perfectly normal) if you are ready to

resume physical intimacy immediately. Many couples find immense healing and comfort in one another's bodies; that is part of the blessing of the relationship God gave us in marriage. But it's also perfectly normal to feel hesitant to engage in physical intimacy too soon after discovering your husband's porn addiction. You may have questions that you want answered before you can make yourself vulnerable in that way, or you may just need space to pray and regroup before you are mentally ready for sex.

The only caution I would give is to remember the words of 1 Corinthians 7:5:

> *Do not deprive one another except with*
> *consent for a time, that you may give your-*
> *selves to fasting and prayer; and come to-*
> *gether again so that Satan does not tempt*
> *you because of your lack of self-control.*

Remember that God gave us sex for our protection against temptations. It is for both your benefit and your husband's. Refraining from sex for a time is not necessarily wrong, but coming together as soon as you are able is a wise step for your marriage.

Again, if need be, start slow. Sex is not the goal. Intimacy is the goal; a close relationship where both you and your husband feel safe and secure. That takes time. As you grow closer together, trust and trustworthiness will naturally grow as well, making physical intimacy easier.

Sex is an important part of healing your marriage. It's also a huge support to your husband's recovery. When there are few opportunities for sexual release, the temptation of porn and masturbation is overwhelming. Your husband needs you physically. A willingness to give yourself to him is one of the greatest ways you can help him remain pure.

It isn't so much the *frequency* of sex that helps a man stay motivated to guard his mind as the *availability* of sex. When a wife communicates her desire for her husband's body and reminds him that she is there for him whenever he wants her, a husband can more easily accept those times when sex is not possible. Even when actual intercourse is not an option (such as right after childbirth), there is still a multitude of ways to show physical affection and offer your husband a degree of sexual satisfaction. It will make it a thousand times easier for him to fight against temptation when he knows you want his body and that you are available to please him.

Interestingly, though, sex is not always the most important aspect of helping your husband stay sexually pure. When I asked Joshua what he thought one of the most helpful things I could do to encourage him in his recovery was, his answer was surprisingly simple. Flirt with him. I was expecting him to say "sex," but for my husband flirting is a big part of what helps him feel secure in our relationship, and therefore less likely to be tempted by porn. It lets him know I'm thinking about him and am happy with our relationship. When he feels secure in our relationship and feels like he's succeeding at making his wife happy, he wants to remain faithful with everything that is in him.

Talking to other men, we have found this to be a common sentiment. It is easier for a man to remember that he wants to please his wife when he feels a reciprocal desire from her. It doesn't have to be sexual in nature. Just a wink and a smile are encouraging. For many men, a flirtatious, appreciative wife goes a long way toward reminding him that he is loved, accepted, and admired. By the same token, a critical, snarky, nagging wife degrades a man's emotional welfare and makes it more difficult for him to reject pornography. It goes back to that low self-esteem issue that makes men vulnerable. When he feels like a failure, he is tempted to search out those digital porn stars who tell him he is actually a big shot.

The aspect of intimacy which most helps your husband stay clean will be specific to your marriage. Communicate with your husband and learn what is most important to him. It may be sex, or it may be affirmation of your respect for him. Cultivating intimacy will help you understand how best to help him in his battle against pornography. It will draw your hearts together as you seek to restore your marriage.

Help Your Husband: Remove Temptations

Nevertheless the high places were not taken away, for as yet the people had not directed

*their hearts to the God of their fathers
(2 Chronicles 20:33).*

When a man is deeply steeped in this addiction, removing every form of pornography from his life can seem like an enormous task. Like the people during King Jehoshaphat's reign, your husband may tell himself he doesn't need to get rid of everything, just the worst things. He might be so desensitized that he doesn't even recognize filth for what it is. He needs your help to get rid of "the high places." Love your husband enough to remove potential triggers without him having to ask.

In contrast to Rachel's reaction, Tonya took a loving approach. The day after Tonya discovered Pete's porn use she went through every room in their home and chunked anything that contained even a hint of sexual immorality. She went through their movie collection and trashed all but a few family-friendly films. She ripped pages out of magazines and deleted sensual songs from their playlists. Tonya did this out of a desire to protect her husband and to make it easier for him to keep his mind pure. She did this because her love for his soul was greater than her love for any material item.

> He shouldn't have to guard his eyes in his own home. This is his safe haven. I'm his helpmeet and I'm here to help him get to Heaven. Why wouldn't I want to remove anything that has the potential to make him stumble?

There have been periods when Tonya has screened all of Pete's email and deleted his spam before he checked for messages. In the beginning, she was the one to get the mail and trash the ads and newspaper articles that contained inappropriate pictures. Now that trust has been rebuilt Tonya is a little less precautious, but it has taken years for Pete to regain her confidence. Pete helped Tonya heal by not complaining about her actions. He appreciated her desire to help him stay pure, and he recognized that this was exactly what he needed. Because of Pete's humble reaction to her vigilance, Tonya gradually found it easier to trust that his heart had truly changed.

Rather than becoming bitter about Pete's need for assistance, Tonya embraced her role of blessing her husband.

> I see myself as the guard of the gate to our little kingdom. It's part of my job to make sure that nothing sexually impure makes its way through that door into our castle. I do this for the sake of my husband, but also for the sake of my children and anyone else who might visit us. I want our home to be a place where eyes don't have to worry about landing on something they have to bounce away from. It doesn't matter where you look in our home. Your eyes and mind are allowed to relax here. This is an oasis for the war-weary.

I love that Tonya has taken an active role as keeper

of the purity of her home. While trashing three-quarters of your movie collection may seem excessive, that's exactly the kind of approach your husband needs to break his porn addiction. Porn is an extremely addictive substance. Extreme measures need to be taken to remove every trace of that substance from your home.

Your husband may not always appreciate your efforts. When someone has an addiction, it's hard for them to see how drastically their lives need to change. Your husband may not even realize a certain thing is causing him a problem until the urge to search for porn takes him by surprise. For instance, a lot of people don't realize how much graphic sensuality most PG-13 movies contain. They think they are mature enough to watch these films (after all, we're all adults here), and they don't realize how much of an influence even brief scenes of immorality have on their subconscious. It may not be until he is alone days later that images from such a movie return to his mind and the insatiable desire to be gratified by a computer screen overwhelms him.

If your husband balks at the things you wish to remove from your home, gently remind him that you are doing this to help him. The one who is addicted doesn't get to make the rules. He never had the right to allow impurity in his home, and now that he has proved himself untrustworthy he no longer gets to make the decisions about what to allow. No matter how sentimental or enjoyable, if you feel that an item is pornographic in some way, you have the right and the responsibility to trash it.

Sometimes it is not a particular item that causes the most temptation but a certain lifestyle or relationship. Getting sensual material out of the home is great, but occasionally you must look beyond the obvious and modify a way of life that has become comfortable. This is when radical change becomes really difficult.

Brenda and William, the newlyweds mentioned in Chapter 3, found that the changes required to break free from porn were sometimes painful. William worked for a company where he occasionally teamed up with Joe for business trips. The two became close friends and they and their wives enjoyed spending time together outside of work. One of their favorite activities was to hang out in front of Joe and Emily's big screen TV. Being the host of these get-togethers, Joe was usually the one to choose the movie. He loved action packed thrillers, and didn't mind a few sex scenes here and there. They "didn't affect" him and he mocked people who couldn't overlook the sensuality and just enjoy the storyline. William tried to insist that these films didn't affect him either, but he would struggle with porn for days afterward.

One weekend while out of town for business, Joe and William went out to eat. Joe made a remark about how good the waitresses looked in their short skirts. William had been trying not to notice. Later that evening Joe relaxed in front of the TV in their room, casually watching what could accurately be described as pornographic shows. William didn't say anything. He fought the temptation to look, but in the end lost his resolve.

Once William became serious about getting clean, he realized he couldn't hang around Joe without being drawn into a serious battle with lust. Though he and Brenda loved both Joe and Emily, they quietly withdrew from the once-close relationship. The loss of friends was painful, but necessary.

Changing old habits can be hard for both you and your husband, especially when it results in altered relationships. But it is worth it! Get rid of as many temptations as possible and help your husband become the man God wants him to be, regardless of the cost.

Help Your Husband: Find an Accountability Partner

Part of the provision God has given for escape includes assistance from other Christians.

> *Brethren, if a man is overtaken in any trespass, you who are spiritual restore such a one in a spirit of gentleness, considering yourself lest you also be tempted (Galatians 6:1).*

Very rarely is a porn addiction overcome without help from other people and a deliberate plan for recovery.

You should not be the only person to hold your husband accountable. That stress is overwhelming in the face of your own recovery. If you wish to receive reports on his online activities, there is nothing wrong with that, but be sure someone else is also receiving the reports and is able to contact your husband should any questionable sites appear.

Your husband needs accountability – an open, honest relationship with someone he will contact every week to discuss his fight against porn. Having someone to talk to who has been there, done that, and found a path to freedom will help keep your husband headed in the right direction. At times of extreme temptation, he should have such a friend on speed dial who will talk him down. This friend will ask tough questions, help form a game plan for success, and point out areas where extra caution is needed.

If your husband wants freedom, this assistance from a committed brother in Christ will be an invaluable resource. However, accountability is only as good as your husband's commitment to purity. When I found out during our engagement that Joshua had started looking at pornography again, I was furious. His accountability partners hadn't held him accountable! What good where they? I expected them to keep Joshua away from pornography. But it doesn't work like that. It wasn't their job to keep Joshua from sin. Only he could do that. Their job was to be there when Joshua wanted help to stay pure. When he didn't, his accountability partners couldn't help him.

As beneficial as an accountability partner can be,

your husband must be careful who he chooses to hold him accountable. There must be real commitment from the other party, or the partnership is pointless. Joshua once asked a friend to receive automatic email reports of everything Joshua searched online and hold him accountable for any inappropriate content. Come to find out too late, this friend never checked that email account. Once Joshua slipped up and realized he wasn't going to be called on it, he gave up fighting. Both you and your husband need to have full confidence that the chosen accountability partner will call out any suspicious activity.

Help Your Husband: Set Safeguards

Supporting your husband means helping him set healthy safeguards. These are not rules you lord over him, but safety nets you help him establish so that when temptation arises, he will have a plan of action. The safeguards you agree on should help give you confidence that your husband is staying pure. Your husband should be willing to do whatever it takes to help you trust him. When that is his goal, he will eagerly comply with any boundaries you request. Nothing you ask of your husband is too much for him to prove his faithfulness, assuming you are not asking him to do anything sinful or asking with unrighteous motivation. As a mentor once told me, "If he's not ready to be told what to do, he's not ready to be free."

If a man is bent on self-gratification, rules won't stop him, but they will help keep a man who is intent on staying clean from slipping into old habits. Remember that you are your husband's helpmeet. This is, as Tonya realized, about helping him get to Heaven. There are no lengths too great when it comes to helping your man stay pure. Do whatever it takes.

Consider implementing these practical safeguards:

Ask your husband daily how he is doing. This daily accountability to you helps keep the lines of communication open, as well as encourages your husband to stay clean.

Install accountability software on all devices. Be sure *all* electronic devices are covered. Joshua and I had Covenant Eyes installed on our computer, but he mostly viewed porn on his phone. Make accountability software for all devices a non-negotiable item in your budget, right below giving to the church and taxes. There are free options out there if your budget is tight. Keep in mind, however, that all software can be circumvented one way or another. Like accountability partners, accountability software is there as a safeguard, not insurance, against porn. It is a deterrent, not a guarantee.

Get rid of the Smartphone. It is best for a man in recovery from a porn addiction to remove internet connection from his phone completely. The best way we have found to do this is to go old-school, using a simple flip phone. Cutting off data is not enough, as most phones are equipped with WiFi and can still connect to open networks. While there are filters and restrictions you can use on a Smartphone, most are easily circumvented.

Set boundaries for when electronics are to be used. In our home, electronics are only to be used when the screen is visible from all sides of the room, and only when I am present. All electronics are placed in a specific spot at night. I hold the passwords to all accounts, and I am aware of every site anyone in the home visits.

Get an accountability partner. As discussed above, an accountability partner is an invaluable asset to your husband's recovery.

Go to bed together. For many men, the time of greatest temptation is at night after everyone else has gone to bed. He's a night owl, or he is heavily involved in gaming or some other activity that bores his wife, so she goes to bed before him, assuming he will follow when he's done. Once she is asleep, he turns on the porn. I can't tell you how many times I've heard this story. An easy way to remove this time of temptation is to go to bed together. Agree on a bedtime and stick to it – together.

Get rid of all books, movies, or anything else with any kind of sexual content. You and your husband must both be diligent about turning off anything that takes a turn toward sensuality. Don't wait to see if the scene will pass quickly, or if that is the only sexual part of the book. Stop it. Get rid of it.

Get rid of the TV. Commercials alone are enough to make television a dangerous pastime for a recovering porn addict. TV is unpredictable. You never know what is going to pop up on the screen. With the likelihood that your husband is struggling with a screen addiction, it's best to cut off TV altogether. You'll find you have more time to focus on your relationship and less temptation to justify things you really shouldn't be watching anyway.

Inform each other of all activities – who, where, and what will be involved. There should be little, if any, time unaccounted for. You should know where your husband is at all times, who he is with, and what he plans on doing. This is especially important if the porn addiction has escalated to the point of sexually acting out. Every conversation with another woman should be public and known to you. There should never be any private discussions or messages between your husband and another woman. The same is true for you and another man. That is common sense in any marriage, but is especially important when trust has been violated.

Pray. Ever and always, pray. Pray daily for your husband's battle. Pray together for your marriage. At every opportunity, pray for God's strength and wisdom.

The changes required to defeat a porn addiction can seem radical to those on the outside. Your decisions might not make sense to anybody else. We found that people, even Christians, could be pretty unsupportive of our efforts to guard our eyes. Sometimes it was because they felt judged by our personal standards, but more often it was because our choices simply baffled them. The thing we had to remember was that we did not have to justify our standards to anyone. We are accountable to God for how we guard our hearts, and we must be willing to do whatever that takes.

These strategies can help your marriage, but don't lose sight of the fact that you cannot keep your husband from sin. I had to come to a point where I was able to accept that Joshua's sins are not my responsibility. In the beginning, I was so stressed about making sure he did everything he was supposed to do that I became a control freak. Allowing myself to step back and release control over every little action Joshua took brought me to a place where I was finally able to find healing. There are things you can do to help your husband, but you must also let go and realize that if he ever falls back into using porn it is his decision to make, not yours. There is nothing you can do that will keep him from pornography if his heart is turned toward sin. In the Day of Judgment, you will stand before Christ and give an account of your sin, not your husband's. You are here to help him, not fix him.

Confession of a Former Porn Addict

There are two things that were crucial for me as I began my battle against porn. Brittany gave me both—and it was at a high cost to her. One was incremental, but one has always been absolute: Trust and Commitment.

Brittany made it clear from the beginning that she wasn't going anywhere. Knowing Brittany would be there no matter what made me realize two more things. First, Brittany was worth keeping at any cost she would ever ask. Second, she was a safe person to be open and honest with. I could let her into my dark and scary world, and she had the fortitude to help me climb out.

The more costly gift Brittany gave me was trust. I had broken her trust far worse than anyone she had ever known. The one she trusted the most betrayed and lied to her. Allowing herself to trust again was one of the hardest things she has ever done. Yet, she found it in herself to find ways to trust me. Small ways at first, maybe, but they grew. She kept working on it because it was not something that was going to come naturally. I had taken her natural trust away, and I could not make her trust me again no matter how hard I tried to be trustworthy. She made herself trust me again by choice.

It seems counterintuitive, but the more Britt trusted me, the more I wanted to be trustworthy. The less she trusted me, the harder it was for me to be honorable. We tend to live up to the expectations of others. I think we understand this concept with children regularly, but we don't always grasp it with adult relationships. I am not sure of all the psychology that goes into this, but the more trust Brittany gives, the harder it is for me to break that trust.

Yes, she trusted me explicitly early in our marriage, and I was violating that trust repeatedly. But now, with a pure heart dedicated to becoming the man

I always should have been, every bit of her increased confidence spurs me on to greater integrity.

Rebuilding trust is a gradual process that takes team effort. It's something of a give and take. When I began to show myself trustworthy, Britt showed me more trust—which motivated me to keep fighting. But I also know that if I hadn't proven myself in a certain area, premature trust would have made it harder for me to be faithful. I would have been tempted again to take advantage of that unearned trust.

I had wanted Brittany to trust me when we got married, but I was not yet ready to give up my sin and be trustworthy. Once I came clean, I didn't want Britt to trust me beyond what I was ready to handle. I didn't want to be left alone in a room with a computer, connected to the internet, and be trusted not to use it wrongly. I still don't because, frankly, given enough hours in that setting, I am fearful I would cease to be trustworthy. Can Britt trust me to work on the internet in the same room as her? Sure. Can she trust me to go to Wal-Mart and not browse the lewd magazine and book section? Yes. Can she trust me with a smartphone with unlimited data sitting in my pocket all the time? Well, not sure about Britt, but I know I haven't regained that level of trust in myself. Trusting does not mean blindly setting your marriage up for failure. Deciding to trust again is an intentional step, but it must be tempered with wisdom, and based on evidence.

Besides trust and commitment, one of the greatest ways Brittany supported me was with honest communication. The less a wife communicates her needs, pain, and trust/distrust, the harder it is for a husband to stay pure. Brittany communicated as best she could about everything she was going through. I knew she was angry, but what affected me the most was how she allowed me to see her pain. Had she only shown me anger I wouldn't have understood the level of damage I had done. But she allowed me to see more than just one side of her emotions. She expressed *how* she hurt and what her doubts and fears were. She explained exactly when, where, why, and how she had trouble trusting me. When Britt let me know she was having greater trouble trusting me, sometimes I could look and see a danger zone I had been blind to. I was able to use that to make sure I wasn't walking the edge, but steering clear of sin, giving it a wide berth. Her encouragement was just as valuable. When she reassured me that she trusted me in a certain area, it drove me to keep on keeping on.

Brittany helped me in so many ways—some of which aggravated me, and that I would not admit were helpful at the time. I thought she was doing them out of some sort of anger (like telling me who my new accountability partner was and giving me no choice – what was that, a threat?). I really didn't see it for the act of love that it was. Brittany was trying to help me stop a sin that I had tenaciously clung to for more than 11 years. Her support (even when I didn't like it) made all the difference.

CHAPTER 9:
HURDLES TO HEALING

Healing from trauma is never a smooth process. There are setbacks, unexpected discoveries, and obstacles that temporarily halt progress. There are the foreseeable hurdles, and then there are the attacks from Satan which take you by surprise. Throughout the healing process, it's essential to keep your focus on the goal: to get to Heaven, and to do your best to help your husband get there with you.

Hurdles to healing can come in all sorts of forms. There is no predicting what your greatest obstacle will be, but there are several pitfalls that are nearly universal to wives of porn addicts: Being distracted by Satan's lies, struggling with low self-esteem, and being tempted in unexpected ways. Awareness of these potential hurdles helps us more successfully overcome them.

Satan's Top 3 Lies

Perhaps the hardest part of recovering from your husband's porn addiction is shutting out the lies that Satan hurls. He knows you well; your vulnerability, your history, your weaknesses. His constant barrage is individually tailored to weaken your resolve to set your mind on things above. There are three lies in particular he loves to tell wives of porn addicts.

1. "You're Overreacting"

This is one of Satan's favorite ways to soften the

edges of pornography, and any sin really. "It's no big deal. You're overreacting." It's just a picture of a fake, airbrushed girl. Why should it bother you? What's the big deal? Satan loves to remind us that looking at porn is an incredibly common and accepted practice in our world today. After all, a man is a man. Satan's calculated whispers haunt your thoughts, "You are crazy for feeling this way. Pornography is normal and shouldn't be a big deal to you."

The fact that your husband has been sexually gratifying himself by looking at other women's naked bodies and mentally using them for his pleasure is a big deal. It is a betrayal of his marriage vows to forsake all others and keep himself for you alone. He isn't cherishing you or honoring you when he seeks pleasure from other women. Husbands and wives should be jealous of the relationship they have with one another in the same way God is jealous over His relationship with us (Deuteronomy 4:23-24). When that relationship is violated, you are right to be distressed. You are right to feel betrayed.

More than that, this is a big deal because pornography is a sin. The Bible is explicit when it comes to how God feels about a man lusting after a woman. Jesus says lust is as serious a sin as having sex outside of marriage. It's so serious that Jesus went on to say in Matthew 5:29:

> *If your right eye causes you to sin, pluck it out and cast it from you; for it is more prof-*

*itable for you that one of your members
perish, than for your whole body to be cast
into hell.*

Viewing pornography is such a big deal that it
would be better for your husband's eyes to be gouged
out than for him to continue in his lust.

The suggestion that you should be okay with your
husband looking at porn is a lie from Hell. His eyes are
to be for you alone, and his thoughts are to be holy.
There is nothing pure or holy about pornography. It's a
big deal because God says it's a big deal.

2. "This is Your Fault"

Another one of Satan's favorite lies is that your
husband's sin is somehow your fault. "If you had been
enough as a wife, your husband wouldn't have been
tempted to look at pornography." Hear me clearly. Your
husband's pornography addiction is not your fault.
There is nothing you did or didn't do that forced him to
lust after other women. There is nothing you can do or
refrain from doing that will keep him from returning to
his addiction in the future. You can offer help and encouragement, but the responsibility of fleeing lust is on
him.

There is no room for blame-shifting. This is not
your fault. Your husband did not turn to porn because
you are not attractive enough. He did not turn to porn
because you are unsubmissive or withheld your body
from him. He turned to pornography because of his own

sin.

In Genesis 3, we have a classic example of the blame game. God asked Adam, "Who told you that you were naked?" What was Adam's response? "The woman whom You gave to be with me, she gave me of the tree, and I ate" (Genesis 3:12). In one sweeping accusation, Adam slides the blame over not only to Eve, but to God Himself. "*You* gave her to be with me..." Eve doesn't take much more responsibility. When it's her turn to answer for her deeds, she shoves the blame right on over to the Serpent, "The Serpent deceived me, and I ate." Both Adam and Eve admitted they ate of the tree, but almost as an afterthought. The first thing out of their mouths is an explanation of how someone else caused them to sin.

Isn't that a common response when we are confronted over sin? "The Devil made me do it." Many try to excuse the sin of pornography by appealing to the nature God gave man, and thereby blame God Himself, "You made me this way! You can't hold me responsible for following my natural instincts." Or they try to blame their wives for some flaw that "made" them need pornography. But God held each individual responsible for his own sin in the Garden. Adam was given the punishment of having to work for his living with toil and sweat. Eve was punished with increased pain in childbearing. The Serpent was cursed with the promise of destruction by the Christ. They were all banished from the Garden because of their own sins. They were not excused because of the sins of another.

Ezekiel 18:4 tells us that the soul that sins shall die. The person who commits sin is responsible for his own actions. You can't get out of the consequences by blaming others. If you have purposefully deprived your husband of sexual satisfaction, if you have been disrespectful, nagging, or unsubmissive, those are sins for which you must repent. But that is not why your husband sinned. Your husband viewed pornography because he made the choice to sin.

3. "Your Marriage is Over"

A third favorite lie from Satan is that your marriage is over; in fact, your entire marriage was a joke from the beginning. You never really knew your husband, and there is no hope because you will never be able to completely trust your husband again.

At the risk of sounding like a broken record, it bears repeating: *There is hope for your marriage!* It's not over. You and your husband can win. Never lose sight of the fact that no relationship is too broken for the hand of the healing Savior.

Your husband's struggle with porn does not necessarily mean he wants out of your marriage. I say "not necessarily" because, sadly, the love of some men has grown cold. Sometimes a man would rather cling to his addiction than save his marriage. Sometimes he listens to Satan's lie that his wife is better off without him and his problems. But there is even hope for those men. There is hope because there is Christ! Christ is patient and not willing that any should perish (2 Peter 3:9, 15).

God is doing everything He can to draw your husband to repentance. He is able to redeem even the most desperate situations.

Your marriage is not over. Some porn addicts do seek a divorce, but this is not the case for the majority of Christian men struggling with porn. They don't want out of the marriage, they want to be free from their bondage to pornography. They love their wives and truly ache over the devastation they have caused. These men can find freedom in Christ. They can rebuild the trust they have destroyed.

Low Self-Esteem

Marie felt like garbage. She blamed herself for Isaac's porn use. After all, those 20 pounds she'd gained since their wedding did feel more like a hundred. Was it really a surprise that he wanted something more? Surveying her body in the mirror, Marie was suddenly indignant. She didn't look that bad! What was wrong with Isaac? Surely plenty of guys would find her more attractive than porn. And yet every time another woman walked by, Marie suddenly felt inadequate. With a sinking feeling, she watched her husband closely. Was he comparing her to that other woman's perfect figure? Looking down at her own flabby thighs, Marie fought back tears. Though it made her feel even more like garbage, she hated every other woman for the beauty she felt she did not possess.

Does this sound familiar?

Poor self-image and negative self-talk torment

thousands of women whose husbands look at porn. They can't get away from their own internal comparisons of themselves with others. Deeply aware of their personal flaws, many women rarely, if ever, feel comfortable revealing themselves in the bedroom. When a husband has been looking at porn, his assurances of his wife's beauty fall flat. In her mind he's already communicated that she's ugly and repulsive by looking at porn in the first place. She internalizes that message and interprets it as, "I am not enough."

When we allow negative self-talk to flood our thoughts, it becomes a way of life. We train ourselves to constantly repeat things like, "I'm such an idiot." "I can't do anything right." "I'm worthless." We speak to ourselves in ways we would never speak to any other of God's creation. The Father doesn't like hearing you criticize yourself in such terms any more than He appreciates you tearing down someone else. Jesus valued you enough to die for you. Whether or not you feel worthy of that love, you cannot argue with His estimation of your worth. To bully yourself is to bully the very person Christ gave His life to love.

The truth is that no matter how perfect you are, you can never be "enough" to keep your husband from sin. Comparing yourself to someone else and wondering if you could have prevented his porn addiction by being more like "so-and-so" is like wondering if you could have stopped the rain by being a giraffe. The two have nothing to do with each other. It's a waste of energy to try to figure out how to be a giraffe. Number one, you can't be anyone other than you. Number two, even if you could, it wouldn't change your husband's sin, because his choice wasn't a result of anything you are or are not.

Despite this knowledge, our bargaining and guilt cause us to try to find some way we are at fault for our husbands' sin. "I didn't pay attention to how stressed he was. I am such a horrible wife." "I pushed him into it by being so critical and impatient." "I'm so boring. No wonder he'd rather spend time with porn than with me." And then there is the final blow to healthy self-esteem, "That woman is everything I'm not. Why can't I be more like her?"

Insecure people naturally compare themselves to others. When your husband is addicted to porn, regardless of whether you know in your head that it is not your fault, it's so easy to compare yourself with other women, especially physically. You fall into a pattern of thinking that if you'd been more beautiful or sexier – like *her* – you wouldn't be dealing with this problem. Looking at it from another perspective might help you avoid this trap. Remind yourself that when you compare your physical appearance to another woman, all you're doing is objectifying both yourself and her. You are chasing what pornography promotes as the highest worth of a woman instead of what God says is priceless.

You are more than an object to look at, and so is the woman with whom you compare yourself. Is her face really her greatest quality? Does it ultimately matter that she has a pretty smile or thin arms? Don't you see deeper into that woman than her skin? When you obsess over another woman's appearance in comparison to your own, you miss seeing her as a whole person; someone with hopes, dreams, fears, and flaws, just like you. You fail to value both yourself and the other woman as unique individuals created by God.

We are all unique. There is always going to be a woman who is more [fill in the blank]. We're not here to be the most beautiful, the most talented, or the most popular woman in the world. That's not what we're about. Comparing yourself to others merely steals your joy and distracts you from the work God has in store for you. "Charm is deceitful and beauty is passing, but a woman who fears the LORD, she shall be praised" (Proverbs 31:30).

Porn damages a woman's self-esteem and makes it hard for her not to compare herself with other women (both in real life and on the porn stage). When you fear you are not enough, it can make it difficult to even be around other women because you view them as a threat. You might resent every woman you perceive as a possible source of temptation to your husband. This jealousy strains your friendships, traps you in isolation, and makes you irrationally suspicious of every person around you. You begin to view other women with jealousy, interacting with them in ways borne of that fear.

As long as you dwell on your flaws and compare

yourself to someone else, your progress toward healing will be hindered. You cannot recover from your husband's porn use when you cling to pornography's core lies – that women are to be prized for their looks and that being sexy is what keeps men happy. Getting over this hurdle to healing requires that you meditate on Truth rather than on what the world says about the importance of physical appearance. Listen to what God says about how valuable you are:

- He valued you enough to carefully form you in your mother's womb (Psalm 139:13-15).
- He cares about every detail of your life, right down to numbering the hairs on your head (Luke 12:6-7).
- He gave His very life for you (John 3:16; Romans 5:8; 1 John 3:16).
- He made a plan to adopt you as His daughter (Ephesians 1:5-6).
- He loves to shower you with good gifts (Matthew 7:11).
- He longs to provide you with rest (Matthew 11:28-30).
- He, the God of Heaven and Earth, chooses to love YOU (1 John 4:19-21).

Replace negative self-talk and comparisons with positive thoughts from the Word. Focus not on striving after physical beauty, but on cultivating a heart that reflects Jesus. That is what God values. "For the LORD does not see as man sees; for man looks at the outward appearance, but the LORD looks at the heart" (1 Samuel 16:7b).

Unexpected Temptation

Satan loves to throw curve balls. Especially in the wake of betrayal, he loves to bring temptation out of (seemingly) nowhere. Things you think will never be a temptation for you suddenly become appealing, leaving you confused and unprepared to handle the situation. While this could be any number of struggles, a common area of temptation for wives of porn addicts ironically involves temptation toward sexual sin.

It often starts out as envy. It seems as if every marriage around you is strong, and it is only your own that is failing. You wonder what makes those couples thrive. What do they have that you don't?

Once envy is stirred, desire awakens. When you compare your marriage to others, it's easy to become convinced that a different man could ease the pain you're going through. Your husband's unfaithfulness leaves a void in your marriage and it is tempting to look to other men to fill that hole. Inappropriate relationships become appealing due to a need for love, a desire to connect emotionally, and sometimes a longing for revenge.

Every marriage has its difficulties, but that is not your business. Your own marriage needs your full attention. Comparing your relationship or your husband to any other leads to discontentment and opens a dangerous door for temptation. Be extra cautious about your interactions with men around you during this time. Give your focus completely to your relationship with your own husband.

It is not only emotional or physical affairs that can become unexpectedly tempting at this time. What comes as a surprise to a large number of wives of porn addicts is how they themselves are now tempted to view pornography. Once begun, they quickly find themselves just as addicted as their husbands.

"Female porn addict" might sound like an oxymoron, but women who seek graphic depictions of sex are becoming strikingly more common, making up one-third of pornography users. Porn was once considered a man's problem, but women are not immune to temptation in this area. Pornography can be appealing to women, particularly wives of porn addicts, for several reasons.

5 Reasons Women Look at Porn

1. Curiosity

It starts the same way for nearly everyone – male, female, child, or adult. Curiosity. We all have an innate desire to know what's behind the curtain. Sometimes wives look at porn because they wonder what their husbands have been viewing. They want to know what is so appealing, so they do a little "research." They want to see the competition and know what they're up against.

2. Inspiration

Pornography engages wives of porn addicts who are looking for ways to get their husbands' attention. Seeing the competition, some women then seek "education" – instruction on how to win their husbands back through sexual favors. Websites which offer false promises of "dirty little secrets" to make your bed more appealing to your husband are nothing more than polished up porn sites themselves.

If you are looking for ways to make intimacy with your husband more satisfying, there are several books I recommend. "The Act of Marriage" by Tim and Beverly LaHaye; "Intended for Pleasure" by Dr. Ed Wheat; and "Sexual Happiness in Marriage" by Herbert J. Miles. Though not written by members of the church, these books all approach the subject with a biblical perspective and handle the topic delicately. They are thorough and descriptive, but not graphic.

3. Arousal

Pornography can be appealing to women who have a hard time getting in the mood for sex. Some foolish counselors even advise couples watch porn together as part of their foreplay if they're having a hard time with arousal. It is tempting for women to turn to porn and masturbation when their husbands are unwilling or unable to satisfy their sexual desires. Porn proposes a quick route to stimulation and a degree of satisfaction without the time and effort it takes to be intimate with your husband.

4. Self-Medication

When a husband's attitudes and actions communicate to his wife that she is worthless in the bedroom, pornography provides a way of escape and self-medication. It offers a secret place to nurse wounds. As women, we are generally more stimulated by the written word than by visual images, so it is the romance novel we find more luring. We fool ourselves into thinking we're reading the book for the storyline or that we're just skimming the sex scenes, but it's really the thrilling escape from reality that we're after. Erotic novels take our minds into a different world where sexual fantasies are explored with abandon. Whether romance novels or graphic images, turning to pornography only leads to more pain.

5. Revenge

Wives of porn addicts sometimes turn to porn themselves out of a desire for revenge. They want their husbands to experience the same pain that they inflicted; so they cheat in the same way. This backfires on multiple levels. First, a husband who is addicted to porn has rewired his brain in such a way as to remove the shock value of finding his wife looking at porn. It is not as offensive to him as it is for his wife to find erotic material on his device. Second, a woman who looks at porn as a tactic for revenge can find herself in a spiral of addiction herself. Third, God never calls us to seek revenge for wrongs done to us. In fact, He says, "Do not say, 'I will recompense evil'; Wait for the LORD, and He will save you" (Proverbs 20:22). It is not your place to punish your husband. Vengeance belongs to the Lord. "For we know Him who said, 'Vengeance is Mine, I will repay,' says the Lord. And again, 'The LORD will judge His people'" (Hebrews 10:30). Your responsibility is to ensure that you are walking purely in His sight.

One woman shared with me her struggle with porn, which started out as mere curiosity. Her husband had struggled with addiction in the past, but it wasn't until her brother's marriage fell apart because of repeated porn use that she wanted to know what was so appealing that it could be worth destroying a relationship.

> "It definitely was a curiosity factor. It was something I had never looked at before. But then I did, and then again days later."

She and her husband already had filtering software installed, but she found the loopholes. For one, she was the creator of the password and could turn the filter off. She also discovered she could find porn on certain sites that were not flagged. She said:

> Be wary of Pinterest. I unintentionally came across porn on there. I don't think it's something the rules say they allow, but people get creative on naming things and unless it's reported it doesn't get taken off.

She went on to describe how her sin affected all areas of her life.

> My whole attitude was affected. I was unusually grumpy and reserved. I felt guilt and shame. My

husband actually found out because of a random search history review and he asked me. I tearfully told him everything and how I had accessed it. I have never felt more vulnerable in my life, but the relief that he knew was huge. And because of his experience he absolutely understood the temptation and was so kind. I try to keep the memory of that night clear as a strengthening reminder to resist the temptation to look at porn again. Being a stay-at-home mom, I have many opportunities to view it. Removing *easy* access is helpful, but not completely possible as long as Smartphones are in the home. If you turn off WiFi on the phone and use data, our filtering software isn't used because it runs through the router. But doing that is one more intentional step that is an opportunity to stop.

If you find yourself tempted to view pornography, take it seriously. Confess your struggle to your husband, and together come up with a plan to address the issue before it becomes a problem. One creative safeguard this couple decided to implement was to each keep half of the internet password. That way, when either of them wants to get online, both have to enter their half of the password first.

Curiosity, sex education, arousal, self-medication, and revenge can lead women into pornography—even though they know at the outset how much pain it brings. Sins which were once abhorrent to you, now become tempting. Carefully guard your heart and mind. Pornography, jealousy over other people's marriages, and inappropriate relationships with other men will only damage your ability to rebuild intimacy with your husband and emotionally heal from his betrayal.

Confessions of a Former Porn Addict

Satan looked for every possible hurdle to toss in my path to keep us from healing—and not just my path, but Brittany's too. When we were open and honest, and shared those struggles with each other, we were able to make progress. If we kept any of it hidden, Satan quickly took advantage of the opportunity to use it against us.

Satan kept putting lies in my head. She's just overreacting, he would say. It's really her fault that you had to find refuge in porn, came the refrain at other times. Your marriage isn't worth keeping anyway—it's already over. Might as well face reality and give up.

I struggled hard against these thoughts. They were appealing, because it took all the blame off me. Sometimes they tainted my words, and actions towards Britt. I needed her help in overcoming these hurdles, by continually pointing me to the truth and the goal that we were working towards. It took (and continues to take) clear thinking, intentional decisions, and dependence on God to fight against those lies.

CHAPTER 10:
PROTECTING THE INNOCENT

Maybe it was just my imagination.

I watched him closely to be sure.

Sitting in the living room of a friend's house, I observed her son scrolling through Netflix in search of something for his younger brother to watch. Up and down he went. Despite the abundance of cartoons and family films available, he couldn't seem to settle on one. He repeatedly scrolled to the top of the page and then to the bottom and then back up again, stopping for a few brief seconds somewhere in the middle, his curser always landing on the same cover picture. Curious, I looked closer. The image that so captivated his attention was an image of a mostly nude woman, sensuously displaying a gun strapped to her side. My young friend was mesmerized. He was nine years old.

When I think about that young boy, accidentally stumbling across a despicable image his innocent mind never should have seen, my heart hurts. Children are so impressionable. An image once seen cannot be unseen. Just one image can set a child on a path to addiction.

As a mother of two baby boys at the time of my husband's confession, one of my biggest concerns was, "Is it even possible to protect my sons from a porn addiction in today's world?" I asked a counselor in desperation, "It seems like every guy I know is struggling with a porn addiction. Is there any man out there who has stayed clean?" His response was that, by the grace of God, he was not struggling with an addiction to porn at that time. He told me he used the wording, "at this time," because he didn't want to be prideful enough to think it could *never* be a temptation for him; but it wasn't *currently* a struggle. And there are many men who have not relinquished control of their minds for a lifetime of bondage. Pornography is a huge temptation, especially for men, but that doesn't mean it is inevitable for your children to be hooked.

Know the Facts

One of the gravest failures of many parents today is neglecting to protect their children from the over-sexualized society in which we live. Many parents may be ignorant of just how bad things have gotten, but *we* cannot afford to remain naïve. Our children's souls are too precious to stick our heads in the sand and pretend that our family is immune to pornography. We've got to know the facts about the environment in which we are raising our kids.

Our children are being exposed to pornography at earlier ages than ever before. When I first began researching the topic in 2013, the average age of exposure was 11 years old. New studies suggest that the average age of exposure is now as young as 8 or 9 years old.[29]

---

[29] "Consider This." Novus Project. www.thenovusproject.org/resource-hub/parents (accessed September 25, 2018).

That's how old my friend's son was when he kept returning to that Netflix movie. Unfortunately, I doubt it was the first time he had noticed such an image. Drive down any interstate and you are bombarded with sexualized billboards. If your kids watch any amount of TV, they've likely already been exposed to sexualized images. Your kids see it everywhere, and they are not oblivious.

Kids see these pictures at younger ages than ever before, but their minds are incapable of understanding what they're seeing. They become hooked on pornography before they even really understand sexuality or what is happening in the images they're viewing. They don't really know what's going on – but they like it, and they keep going back for more.

We all know children are sponges. They soak up everything, especially any new experience, and they retain those memories for decades. My husband remembers the first time he saw an image of a naked woman. It is burned into his memory and he can see it just as clearly today as the day he was exposed. Part of that is because he is a man, and men have an outstanding capability for visual recall. That is intensified by the fact that he saw the image as a young boy. I can remember the first time I saw nudity on TV, too. I was seven years old, but I can clearly recall the details, right down to the color of the jacket someone was wearing in the background. Children's brains are wired to remember new, shocking events. If the questions raised by such images are not answered satisfactorily, their curiosity will lead them to investigate on their own.

The Sad Facts[30]:

- 93% of boys and 62% of girls are exposed to internet pornography before the age of 18
- 70% of boys have spent more than 30 consecutive minutes looking at online pornography on at least one occasion. 35% of boys have done this on more than ten occasions
- 23% of girls have spent more than 30 consecutive minutes looking at online pornography on at least one occasion. 14% of girls have done this on more than one occasion
- 83% of boys and 57% of girls have viewed group sex on the internet
- 69% of boys and 55% of girls have seen pornography depicting same-sex intercourse
- 39% of boys and 23% of girls have seen online sex acts depicting bondage
- 32% of boys and 18% of girls have viewed bestiality on the internet
- 18% of boys and 10% of girls have seen depictions of rape and/or sexual violence on the internet
- 15% of boys and 9% of girls have seen child

---

[30] "A Parent's Primer on internet Pornography." www.digitalkidsinitiative.com/wp-content/uploads/2016/09/ Parent_Primer_Internet_Pornography-Revised-September-2016.pdf (accessed September 25, 2018).

pornography
- The 12-17 year-old age group is the largest consumer of internet pornography

Are you shocked? I cried the first time I read those statistics. Nearly 100% of our boys have been exposed to online pornography before the age of 18 years old! And it was painfully eye-opening to see that our girls are at risk in equally increasing rates. This is the world in which we live. The question these days is not, "Will my child see pornography?" but, "How will my child react when he or she is exposed?"

If you have a child over the age of nine, he or she has likely already been exposed to pornography. How? Most parents are shocked to learn where their children were first exposed to pornography. According to the studies:

- 4 out of 5 children with an email address regularly receive pornographic spam[31]
- 20% of children have received sexual solicitation[32]
- 90% of children between the ages of 8-16 have been exposed to porn, and most of those were

---

[31] "Children Upset by Spam E-mail." BBC News. http://news.bbc.co.uk/2/hi/technology/2978134.stm (accessed September 25, 2018).
[32] "Internet Pornography Statistics." My Kids Browser. www.mykidsbrowser.com/pornography_stats.php (accessed September 25, 2018).

exposed while doing homework[33]

The majority of homework research takes place on the internet. Unfortunately, that is how a large percentage of children stumble into the world of pornography. Being aware of what your kids are doing online means more than just knowing they are doing homework. You need to know exactly what they are viewing online at all times. Have your family computer set up in a high traffic area, and only allow your children online access under your supervision. It's not a matter of your child being untrustworthy; it's a matter of protecting him from the attacks of Satan.

The *Journal of Adolescent Health* found that when youth are exposed to porn they demonstrate:

1. An exaggerated perception of sex in society
2. Diminished trust between couples
3. An abandonment of hope for monogamy
4. The belief that promiscuity is the natural state
5. The belief that abstinence is unhealthy and abnormal
6. The belief that marriage is confining (cynicism)
7. A lack of attraction to raising a family[34]

An addiction to pornography has lifelong effects on the health of children, both physically and psycho-

---

[33] Ibid.

[34] Zillmann, Dolf. "Influence of Unrestrained Access to Erotica on Adolescents' and Young Adults' Dispositions toward Sexuality." *Journal of Adolescent Health* Volume 27 (2000): Pages 41-44

logically. Therapists now say that exposure to porn is the equivalent of being mentally molested – an emotional trauma that lasts a lifetime. In addition, the rate of teen pregnancy is twice as high among those frequently exposed to porn.

Why Kids Look at Porn

The top reason kids start looking at porn is, again, curiosity. Children are naturally curious. Their favorite question is, "Why?" My five-year-old can ask an average of 3.2 million questions per second (give or take a few million). He wants to know everything there is to know about the world, and if I don't have the answer, he's going to go looking.

When a child sees an image of something he's never seen before, he will want to look at it again to learn more. "What's going on in that picture? Why did my parents freak out when I saw it? Why does my older brother hide the fact that he's looking at these pictures online? Does every naked person look like that?" There is no sexual draw for him at this point. He's just genuinely curious to know what's going on in the picture. It is then he realizes that looking at these pictures gives him a pleasurable feeling. He's not sure why, but he knows he likes that feeling. He returns to the picture, or looks for similar pictures. It doesn't take long before he's hooked.

A second, similar reason kids look at pornography is for sex education. In many homes, sex is a taboo topic, at least until the teenage years. Often parents don't realize how young the questions begin. Kids, who get the feeling their parents don't want to talk about sex, will go searching for the answers themselves. Their young friends willingly introduce them to the world of online education. Or they might go old-school and figure it out for themselves by flipping through books at the library when their parents aren't looking.

If you don't answer your child's questions about sex and human anatomy, someone else will. You've got to be sure you're the one to answer those questions first so that, when he runs into an exhibit on the topic, he's not quite as curious because he already knows what's going on. That's not to say he won't check to make sure you were right, but a lot of his questions will already be answered, and the temptation to hide his interest from you will be lessened. He should know he is free to ask you anything and doesn't have to be ashamed of his questions.

Talk to your kids from young ages about where babies come from, how men and women are different physically, what God's plan is for the sexual union. I'm certainly not saying you should sit your five-year-old down and explicitly explain how intercourse works, but I am saying don't leave out that information until he's thirteen. By then, he probably doesn't need you to tell him what's what. He's already figured it out.

Make sex education a normal topic in your home. Little by little, answer their questions as they come. Sometimes parents are unaware they've left their kids with the impression that sex is a "bad" topic simply by waiting for them to come with questions. Be sure you and your husband are the ones to bring it up, frequently, and ask if your children want to know anything specific. Don't make it a big ordeal. In small doses, you can educate your kids in age-appropriate ways.

A third reason kids look at pornography is peer pressure. Their friends are looking at it. Their friends are offering to let them look at it. And if they don't look at it, they become "that kid." That kid who is so sheltered. That kid who has no experience in the real world. That kid who is the only one who doesn't know what a naked girl (or boy) looks like.

Don't expect your child to be the strong, positive influence, withstanding temptation at all times. No matter how mature he is, he is susceptible to the influence of those he associates with. Be the Helicopter Mom. It's okay. Your child's soul is worth it. Know who your kids' friends are, who else will be present when they are hanging out, and what they will be doing. You need to not only know the parents of your child's friends, but also any siblings or other adults who live in the house, and whether there will be an uncle, aunt, or grandparent over while your child is there. One of the most frequent places for kids to be exposed to pornography is during sleepovers. If you are going to allow sleepovers (which I don't recommend) it's best to only permit them at your house where you can limit the use of all electronics.

Curiosity, sex education, and peer pressure are three big reasons kids seek pornography. Aside from the nature of addiction and dopamine release, which we've already discussed, sometimes children will continue to pursue pornography because they are looking for love. They need affirmation, and that man or woman on the screen tells them they are important. They feel sophisticated, and the approval they imagine they receive from a porn star (temporarily) covers a lot of wounds.

Kids need constant affirmation that they are worthy of time and affection. This is something I'm not especially good at. I'm not a particularly touchy person, so it takes work to remember to shower my daughter in hugs and praise. I have to frequently remind myself that my boys need affection even if they squirm away and pretend to wipe off my kisses. I was told by an attachment specialist once that a person needs no less than 12 hugs a day to thrive emotionally. With six kids in our household, that means a lot of loving! For a mama who likes her space, it can be difficult. But if I don't wrap my arms around my kids and assure them that they are loved, approved of, and protected, they will seek to fill that void somewhere else, and it will usually end up being in places that will lead them away from God.

When Your Child Looks at Porn

The distraught mother barely held back tears as she confided that she just didn't feel she could support her son's decision to go to preaching school. I was surprised. I knew my friend had previously been excited about the interest Luke had shown in becoming a Gospel preacher and had encouraged it as a worthy position. What changed?

"I just don't feel like he is worthy to be a preacher. He's just not Christ-like enough. Not good enough to represent the church."

"No preacher is perfect," I reminded her. "Joshua is a good man, but he still sins. We all do!"

"Yes," she replied, "But he is such a strong Christian. My boy has a good heart, but he struggles. I'm sure Joshua would never even think about doing the kind of thing my son has done."

I suddenly had an inkling of what her son was struggling with. Knowing Joshua wouldn't mind, I shared a glimpse into his past. "Joshua is a dedicated Christian, but he's got history like everyone else. He has not made it this far without scars along the way. Like most young men, he struggled for a long time to control his eyes."

My friend's eyes widened with a mixture of shock and relief, "Really?"

"Yes. He's fought very hard to overcome pornography, but it was an addiction for years."

From there my friend poured out her anguish over discovering Luke's pornography use. She shared her heartbreak, her feelings of failure, and her fear that her son had been ruined. She was sure he was now totally unfit for service in the Kingdom. She looked at me with haunted, guilt-ridden eyes. Silent sobs tore at her heart. She had poured so much into her son, but now it seemed as though nothing she had tried to instill in him was working. Like many mothers who have discovered that their innocent little boys have grown into young men with uncontrolled lust, she looked back over her childrearing years and wondered, "What did I do wrong? What did I miss?"

My heart ached for her. When another adult looks at porn, there is an understanding that it was his or her own choice to sin. But when your child looks at porn, there is an overwhelming sense of responsibility. One mother told me, "I've never been so ashamed of myself. I know it wasn't my fault. But... It is."

The downward spiral of self-doubt quickly turns to self-loathing as these mothers try to pinpoint where they went wrong in their parenting. This in turn leads them into deep regret and depression. They don't know what happened. They tried everything they knew to protect their kids. It didn't work. If that didn't work, the rest of their parenting must be worthless, too. Or, so Satan tells them.

While there are certainly things we can do as mothers to help our children guard their hearts and eyes, each person is responsible for his own sin (Ezekiel 18:20). Ultimately, it was your child's choice to continue to view pornography. It's important to allow yourself to process your emotions and reflect on changes to be made, but at some point you must step back and take a breath. We serve a God of Redemption. He has not given up on your son or daughter. Neither can you.

I sit here snuggling my two-year-old son. As I rock him and rub his chubby arms, look into his big, innocent brown eyes, and smell the wafting aroma of his stinky diaper, I simply cannot imagine this child falling into the sin of lust and sexual perversion. It hurts to even consider the possibility, and I cry out to God to guard my baby's soul. The reality of this world is that this boy will face a barrage of temptation from all sides. Our culture is saturated with immorality, and he likely will struggle to keep his eyes on Christ.

This little one. This precious, stinky boy of mine. He will grow. And he will struggle. When he does, how will I help him? How will I show him the way back to God? How will I assure him that God's grace and forgiveness are bigger than his past?

I'm thankful for Joshua's mama who taught him that his past does not own him. Your child's past choices do not own him, either. You have not failed as a mother. Your work is not destroyed. God can use your child's history for good. He needs you to be a reflection of His tender mercy and to show your child that his story doesn't have to end in defeat. Give your child courage and hope that tomorrow can be different.

Ways to Protect Your Children

If we are not aware of the dangers pornography

poses to our kids, we risk losing them to a world which is more than happy to "educate" them. It doesn't matter how righteous your home is, or how many talks you've had with them about keeping their eyes pure. It doesn't matter if you're a preacher's family, an elder's family, or a deacon's family; it doesn't matter whether they go to public, private, or home school. It's not a matter of trust or how responsible your kid is. No family – and no kid – is immune to the power of pornography. It takes constant vigilance, frequent conversations, and a whole lot of prayer to keep your kids safe.

Satan is aggressively seeking the minds of our youth. Addictions started young are all the harder to break. This is a spiritual battle for the souls of our children. We must be smart about protecting them. While they are young, set eternity in their hearts and teach them not only to guard their minds, but how to return to the Father when they stray.

Talk to Them

The most important thing you can do to keep your children safe is to stay connected with them. Talk with them, not just about the dangers of pornography, but about what healthy relationships look like. Spend time getting to know them as individuals. Be present in their lives. Parental communication is vital to shielding our children, and that means communication in all areas of life. It's going to take more than a couple hours a day with your children to teach them about true love, respect, and purity. Integrity is not a weekend conversation, it's a lifetime dialogue. You've got to be the one they look to for help in navigating the waters of sexuality, which means you've got to build their trust in you. You've got to have their hearts.

Talk to your children. Educate them. Answer their questions, regardless of how awkward it feels. If you don't get embarrassed when talking about sexual matters, they likely won't either. Frequently talk to them about what they're going to do when they see something they shouldn't. Teach them to bounce their eyes, and make sure they know to tell you every time they've seen something they had to look away from.

Some have expressed concern that if we often talk to our children about averting their eyes or avoiding situations where they are likely to see immodesty flaunted, then we inadvertently teach them disdain for men or women who are less than modest. This is a legitimate concern if you are not careful to also teach your children to value others. You can teach your children to guard their eyes while still teaching them respect for immodestly dressed people. We teach our children that an undressed person needs privacy. I tell them, "She may not realize this, but she left the house without enough clothes, and we need to respect her enough to give her the privacy she needs." You do not have to go into a long tirade of shaming the woman. Simply teach your children their own responsibility when they see a man or woman dressed immodestly.

Train Them Practically

Train your children from an early age to avert their eyes. Teaching our kids to bounce their eyes started early in our home. My oldest was three at the time, and his younger brother was two. We played a game where I trained them to either close their eyes or look in the opposite direction every time I said, "Turn your eyes, boys." That was our key phrase. We practiced multiple times a day, at random points. I made it fun, used silly voices, and gave them loud praise when they obeyed. Sometimes I used something innocent, like a stuffed animal, and told them that whenever I said, "Turn your eyes," they were to avoid looking at that beloved toy until I told them it was okay again. Now whenever I see something my children don't need to see, I simply say, "Turn your eyes, kids," and they look in another direction or close their eyes until I assure them it's safe. As they've grown, they've started to learn when to avert their eyes without prompting. They'll turn their heads and search for eye contact with me, and then we smile at each other until I give them the "Okay."

At some point when your child is on the computer, he will run into something he should not see. Teach him how to respond. Teach your children why spam is dangerous and should never be opened. Show them how to quickly exit a computer screen and completely shut down the system when something inappropriate pops up, and train them to then immediately come tell you.

Give your child the gift of wisdom to avoid the harlots of pornography. Warn them not to take that first step, and to stay away from her corner. Instruct them that pornography is a seductress whose "house is the way to Hell" (Proverbs 7:27). Pray for and train your child so that he does not end up like the fool in Proverbs 7:6-8.

> *For at the window of my house I looked through my lattice, and saw among the simple, I perceived among the youths a young man devoid of understanding, passing along the street near her corner; and he took the path to her house.*

Teach your children to stay away from her street.

Be Consistent

Teach your kids to bounce their eyes in all areas of life. There is no situation where it's okay for boys and girls to engage in recreation that involves anyone being underdressed. Dancing, swimming, cheerleading, volleyball and other sports – these all usually involve exposure of skin that your kids need to avoid. Be consistent. If it's not okay to look at girls in miniskirts online, it's not okay to watch them parade in cheer outfits. A beach populated with bikinis and bare chests is no place for Christians. As Cindy Colley said in a lesson on protecting your children from pornography, "Your boys are not going to understand your hypocrisy." Our children see our inconsistencies. If you make excuses for partaking in activities that glorify immodesty, they will follow your lead further than you meant to go.

Limit Screen Time

According to the American Academy of Pediatrics, the average child spends seven hours a day looking at a computer screen of some type.[35] By the time your child gets home from school, where electronics are used for education, his brain is already on digital overload. Your child's mind needs time to reset so he can focus and function in the world apart from a screen. It is wise to limit his use of electronics as recreation.

As we talked about earlier, screens are addictive and can physically alter the brain before it is even permanently molded. They can also aggravate behavioral problems due to overstimulation. This is why restricting screen time as a punishment for bad behavior is effective for children. It's not just taking away something the child enjoys; it's giving his brain a chance to reset and rewire. He is coming down off of a high of overstimulation and, given enough time, he is better able to regulate his actions again. (As a side note, quick rewards and fast-paced challenges will help your child come off of a screen high).

Delay the introduction of digital devices as long as possible. I know that when your kids are wild and you're on a deadline, it's easy to allow a movie to babysit your little ones. I've done it myself! Occasion-

---

[35] "Media and Children Communication Toolkit." American Academy of Pediatrics. www.aap.org/en-us/advocacy-and-policy/aap-health-initiatives/Pages/Media-and-Children.aspx (accessed September 25, 2018).

ally using devices as a sanity saver for Mama is not wrong. Using technology purposefully and wisely is one thing, but allowing your kids unrestricted access to digital devices sets them up for screen addiction, leading to a faster fall into pornography. Be wise about how and when you allow access to electronics.

Your kids don't need the newest gadget on the block. Smartphones are unnecessary. If they're going to have a cell phone for emergencies, a flip phone is all that is needed. Homework should be done on the family computer in the living room with someone else present. There is no need for a child to be alone with electronic devices, especially not behind closed doors or after everyone else has gone to bed. Be sure that all phones, iPads, laptops, and other devices are turned in before bedtime, and keep them in your room where the child will not have access to them throughout the night. Your child (or anyone else for that matter) does not need his phone during meal times, Bible class, or worship. Replace electronics with open communication, Bible time, family discussion, reading aloud, and game nights.

Above all, enforce the concept that your child has no privacy rights. This should be understood by all family members. You, the parent, should have access to all passwords, accounts, apps, social media pages, etc. Parents are responsible for how and when their children use electronics. We must diligently guard our children's hearts.

Install Software

Install accountability and filtering software on all devices. Blocking certain sites or keywords is not enough. While filtering content is important, there are easy ways to get around those systems. Choose accountability software that will record every online action and send a report to your email. Keep all passwords (both to your email address and accountability software) from your children.

We currently use Covenant Eyes on our devices, but you will want to research the safest and best option for your family. OpenDNS Family Shield is an excellent (and free!) filtering system that blocks inappropriate content at the router level. A few other companies you may want to look into are Integrity Online, Accountable2You, Safe Eyes, Net Nanny, and Ever Accountable. Keep in mind that not all software works well on all devices, so do your research before you invest.

Once you have installed software, remember to view the reports! It is sad how many kids view pornography in spite of filters, knowing that their parents never view the records. Accountability software is useless if you do not consistently monitor the activity. So many people have continued in porn for years without being caught, simply because accountability partners, parents, and spouses never bothered to actually look at the reports.

Be careful not to let your children know the details

about how you monitor their internet usage. Our children need to know that we are aware of their online activities, but exactly how we know should not be disclosed. If your children know exactly how you're monitoring their activity, trust me, they can find a way around it. If we have to approach one of our children about things they have been doing online, the emphasis should be on opening communication about making decisions that are pleasing to God. Exactly how we came to the knowledge of their breach should remain confidential for their own protection.

Be Savvy

Relentlessly research every app your child uses. There are thousands of apps to download that were created with harmless intentions, but which predators use to prey on children. Be particularly leery of games like Minecraft, which uses data to give players the ability to connect with strangers over the internet. I recommend avoiding apps and internet games for your kids altogether, but if they do use data on their devices, be conscious of the dangers and block apps that were created specifically for sexual exploits.

The official descriptions on some of these apps sound harmless enough, but be aware of how they are used to spread pornography and draw children into sexual encounters. A few dangerous apps to be aware of include:

- **Omegle** – Allows users to socialize with strangers and does not require registration. This app randomly pairs users in a one-on-one chat room setting that includes a video conferencing feature.

- **Hot or Not** – Used to rate the attractiveness of people in uploaded photos (specifies that the photos are uploaded voluntarily, but there is no way of regulating whether someone uploads a picture of somebody else).
- **Down Dating** – Casual dating app, formerly known as "Bang with Friends." More like a casual sex app, Down allows you to hook up with strangers and friends alike near your location.
- **Serahah** – Designed as a way to get "honest feedback from your coworkers and friends," this app allows users to send anonymous messages.

These are just a few of the apps designed specifically for adult content, but keep in mind that an app or website does not have to have a "Mature" rating to allow access to pornography. Pinterest, an innocent favorite of moms everywhere, is one easy place to access illicit photos. While porn is against Pinterest's policies, it's easily uploaded and viewed.

This is true of all social media sites. Understand how these websites work and the potential they present for both pornography and secretive behavior. Being a Facebook friend with your child is not enough. Account settings allow users to block certain people on a friends list from seeing certain posts while still allowing them to see others. In addition, secret accounts are easily created. Don't assume you are seeing everything your children do on Facebook just because you are on their friends list.

Twitter, another social media site, has policies which specify that porn is not allowed on the site and encourages users to report graphic content. However, keeping porn off the site is almost impossible. Accidently clicking onto a pornographic picture or purposefully searching for such is too easy. While porn is against Twitter's policies, they almost never take action against it due to their desire to refrain from censorship. It is your job as a parent to be the censor. Twitter makes that job incredibly difficult.

Be leery of Instagram, a "simple, fun and creative way to capture, edit and share photos and videos." It is a social media app similar to Facebook, but with an emphasis on visual sharing. Are your warning bells going off? While you can monitor who your child is following on Instagram, you cannot restrict what he searches. Pornographic pictures are, unfortunately, easy to find.

Snapchat, created to share multimedia messages, is another popular app which can get your kids into trouble. The principle idea of Snapchat is that pictures and messages are only available for a short time before they disappear. An image can be uploaded, and then vanish before a parent ever knew it existed. Snapchat also now features short video clip capabilities. While pictures and videos do completely vanish from your phone, they can be stored on Snapchat's servers for up to 30 days.

While the user may believe that an inappropriate picture is gone forever, there is a potential for hackers to obtain a copy and use it for evil.

Even more appalling, in May 2018 Snapchat released "Cosmo After Dark." This channel was self-described as "an X-rated weekly edition that goes live every Friday at 6 p.m. and is exclusively dedicated to all things hot and horny." If your child had Snapchat at that time, you could not block this channel. It was one click away. Thankfully, due to the uproar of thousands of parents, this channel was canceled after only one week. But you see how much Snapchat cares about protecting your children, don't you? As far as they are concerned, pornography is acceptable.

Not only do these apps and social media sites have the potential to introduce your child to pornography and objectification of other people, they also encourage self-objectification as well. They encourage you to market yourself to gain "likes." I certainly do not condemn the use of social media sites or image sharing apps, but parents need to be hypersensitive to the ways these can be perverted to exploit children and induce porn addictions. Allowing your child unrestricted access to these sites, and simply warning him not to view the X-rated content, is like sticking a porn magazine in his hand and telling him to only look at the safe pictures. We can, and must, do better.

Preparing Your Daughters

When Joshua and I began courting, he told me he

had struggled with a porn addiction. To some degree, I was prepared for this confession. I wasn't naïve about how prevalent pornography is in our society, even within the church. I had seen the devastation this sin wreaked in relationships around me. What I was not prepared for was how Joshua's history of porn use would affect our relationship, even before he returned to it later in our marriage. I figured history was history. But even before Joshua resumed his addiction, the fact that he had given into the temptation as a single man had negative effects on our relationship.

Many counselors have recommended that if your boyfriend confesses an addiction to porn, you shouldn't marry him. The advice from one counselor is, "If a guy you're dating struggles with this, it will be a life-long struggle. Relapse is not the exception. Do not marry that man." I understand where such advice is coming from. The impact is life long, and most people underestimate the impact of a history of porn use, even after the addiction has been broken. I hesitate to recommend that a girl refuse to date anyone who has ever struggled with porn addiction, mainly because she would be hard-pressed to ever find such a young man in today's world. They do exist. I don't want to come across as believing porn is inevitable for all men, but I do believe we need to prepare our daughters for the strong possibility that the man she marries will have a history of porn use.

Talk to your daughter about pornography and the damage it causes to marriage. Teach her that she does not have the power to keep a man from sinning, that it has nothing to do with her as a person, but everything to do with his lust. When she begins a relationship, get to know the young man she is dating, and ask him these uncomfortable questions: Has he ever looked at pornography? If so, how long has it been since he last viewed it? What safeguards does he have in place to protect himself? Who is holding him accountable for his purity? A young man who is involved with porn will not be able to love your daughter well. It is your job to help protect her from a lifetime of misery.

A history of pornography will affect her marriage, even if the young man stopped well before she ever started dating him. The knowledge that it has been a problem in the past can make your daughter feel insecure and suspicious, which strains communication and trust in marriage. No matter how far removed the addiction, it still has negative consequences, and both your daughter and her boyfriend need to be prepared for that.

Teach your daughter to look for red flags and help her identify them. These include being lax in his entertainment choices, enjoying immodest activities, and showing a lack of modesty himself. Irritation over being interrupted when he's looking at his phone, or insisting he take his phone to the bathroom can also be red flags. Objectification of women, pressuring increased physical contact, and lying are bright red flags!

Be involved in your daughter's relationships, get to know every young man she's interested in, and ask the embarrassing questions. It is quite possible he will have struggled with porn. That relationship doesn't necessarily have to be over, but the young man should be given a specified amount of time to prove himself before you give your blessing to his relationship with your daughter. Your daughter needs to know that while there is forgiveness for every sin, there are some sins which bring heavier baggage into marriage, and which require special care to ensure they stay out of the relationship permanently.

The Hope of Tomorrow

Pornography use is not the Unforgiveable Sin. If your child begins down the path to a porn addiction, redirection is possible. You cannot make every choice for your child. He makes the decision for himself whether or not to look at pornography. You are not a failure as a mother if your teenager decides to immerse himself in this sin. We cannot ensure 100% that our kids will stay pure, but there's a lot of things we can do to stand against pornography's invasion into our homes. Be upfront in teaching your children the dangers of the world. Set safeguards and restrictions. And don't underestimate the power of prayer (James 5:16).

Above all, you've got to guide your child's heart. Children always seem to know more about electronics than their parents. No matter what guards you put in place, if they want to find a way to access things they shouldn't, they will. If nothing else, there's always a friend's digital device. You cannot always keep evil away from them. This is why you must train them how to shun evil. Your children need to know the importance of guarding their own hearts. They need to understand the dangerous consequences of allowing filth to taint their minds. I believe the best method of accomplishing this is by being open about how your own sin has hurt you and those around you. You should also point out how sins recorded for us in the Bible hurt everyone involved. Don't speak in vague generalities. Be specific, but age appropriate. Impress upon them the addictive abilities of pornography. Point out examples of how this sin has destroyed relationships. Make purity of heart and mind a frequent topic of conversation. No amount of filtering can replace your wise instruction on how to guard their hearts.

Confessions of a Former Porn Addict

It is my responsibility as a parent to guard my children. To an extent, that includes shielding them from temptation. I cannot and should not protect them from all temptation. Sometimes I watch my children being tempted and wait, keeping an eye out, praying they make the right choice. They don't need to know I am watching, ready to stop their actions if they choose to follow the temptation, because they need to build strength to resist Satan on their own. They need to realize that it is truly on them to decide if they will be faithful to God or not. This begins long before they ever have a clear concept of right and wrong. But I also try to make sure some temptations are not constantly blaring in their faces, because I know they are not yet ready to resist.

Monitoring and enforcing limits on internet usage isn't about our children being untrustworthy, it's about them being vulnerable. One reason I fell so completely into temptation was because I had full access to anything on the internet, anytime I wanted. There was a computer in my room connected to the internet and no explicit rules for when it could be used. I was 15 or 16 by this time, but I was in no way ready for that level of temptation. Even the most mature children are vulnerable to the temptations that come from unlimited internet access.

There really wasn't any need for me to be connected to the internet for extended periods of time. I wasn't able to control my screen time, and I know I'm not alone in that struggle. That is why I am so determined to make sure internet limits are enforced with our kids until such time as they have enough self-discipline to control their internet habits themselves.

CHAPTER 11:
IS PORNOGRAPHY CAUSE
FOR DIVORCE?

It is one of the most frequent questions on pornography we receive. "Does my husband's pornography use give me a scriptural right to divorce?" As difficult as it is at a time like this, let's try to consider this question objectively. Our conclusion must not be based on how we feel or what friends say, but on what God says on the topic.

According to the Bible, is pornography cause for divorce? To be perfectly honest, I hate this question! It ignores the more pressing matter, the investigation of which would save far more heartbreak than this question ever will. We need to be asking (and I hope this book helps answer), "How can we build a God-honoring marriage out of this sinful wreck in which we find ourselves?" How can I love my husband more? How can I help him through this sin? How can we demonstrate Christ to our children? How can I be God's woman when Satan has invaded my home and so successfully attacked the one to whom I submit? The important question is not, "Can I divorce him now?" but, "How can we avoid divorce at all cost?"

Satan loves to spout all sorts of lies about how horrific your marriage is and how excellent the "right" marriage could be. Make no mistake. There is no marriage out there that could be better for you than your first marriage, where both you and your husband wholeheartedly turn to God. Satan will whisper lies to the contrary, but remember that's exactly what they are – lies! God hates when man puts asunder that which He joined together (Malachi 2:16), therefore Satan hates God's ideal of one man for one woman for life. The "father of lies" will tell you anything he can to get you to dissolve this union. But God has a bigger, more fulfilling plan.

The Cause of Divorce

Study after study has attempted to determine the most common cause of divorce in societies throughout history. The specific findings of those studies are interesting. However, if we look at it honestly, that which causes divorce hasn't changed since the beginning. The leading cause of divorce in our country, the world, and throughout all time is this: People are giving up! The main reason for divorce is that at least one man or one woman decided that "till death do we part" was just a line, or perhaps even a blatant lie.

We need to take the biblical teaching about covenants very seriously. You made a vow to the man who is now your husband to "love, honor, and cherish," him "through richer or poorer, in sickness and in health, for better or for worse, till death." As Christians we know the sickness experienced in marriage is sometimes of a spiritual nature. We have promised to stick by our spouses despite their struggles with spiritual illness.

> But, he broke our wedding vows! By viewing pornography, he did not keep his whole body for me and me alone. He did not love, honor, or cherish me while he viewed that trash! He's the one who broke our covenant, therefore he has dissolved our marriage vows and I am free.

I can't tell you the number of times I have heard this rather hypocritical argument. Haven't we all broken those vows at one time or another? To my shame, there have been times in our marriage when I have not honored Joshua. There have been times when I have not loved him or cherished him as I ought. This does not dissolve my vows or make the part where I promised to stay with him until death invalid. Nor does it absolve Joshua of the covenant he made to me.

You made a vow for life. Now is the test of your "till death" promise. Your husband isn't dead and (despite the fact that it may have crossed your mind) you aren't going to kill him. "Till death do you part" still applies, and if you are both seeking God above all you can figure out how to glorify Him in marriage together. You can do more than just survive as two roommates who share living quarters. You can thrive as two souls, heaven bound and determined to follow through with all of God's commands to the best of your ability. You can rebuild your home according to God's plans.

All that said, I guess we should answer our most frequently asked question. Is pornography a scriptural cause for divorce? Can I be within God's plan and divorce my husband for his sin of pornography use?

The Bible Speaks

Recall the definitions we looked at in Chapter 2 from Webster's and the Britannica Encyclopedia. Pornography is, "Art with obscene or unchaste treatment or subjects," and, "The presentation of sexual behavior in books, pictures, films, or other media solely to cause sexual excitement." Or, you could use the definition we gave a few paragraphs later in the same chapter, "Any media (words, images, sculpture, video, sounds, etc.) that, as part of its design or nature, causes sexual arousal for someone or something other than one's spouse."

Now that we've refreshed our memory on pornography's definition, let's look at what the Bible says is an acceptable reason for divorce. The main passages that deal with divorce are Matthew 5:31-32, Matthew 19:3-9, and the parallel passages Mark 10:11-12 and Luke 16:18.

Mark and Luke are short and sweet:

> *So He said to them, "Whoever divorces his wife and marries another commits adultery against her. And if a woman divorces her husband and marries another, she commits adultery" (Mark 10:11-12).*

> *Whoever divorces his wife and marries another commits adultery; and whoever marries her who is divorced from her husband commits adultery (Luke 16:18).*

If you read only these two passages, you come away with the idea that divorce and remarriage is sinful. Period. However, in Matthew, Jesus gives allowance for one exception.

> *Furthermore it has been said, "Whoever divorces his wife, let him give her a certificate of divorce." But I say to you that whoever divorces his wife for any reason except sexual immorality causes her to commit adultery; and whoever marries a woman who is divorced commits adultery (Matthew 5:31-32).*

> *He said to them, "Moses, because of the hardness of your hearts, permitted you to divorce your wives, but from the beginning it was not so. And I say to you, whoever divorces his wife, except for sexual immorality, and marries another, commits adultery; and whoever marries her who is divorced commits adultery" (Matthew 19:8-9).*

The Bible gives one reason and one reason only for seeking divorce. What is the one exception God gives to His law against divorce? According to the NKJV quoted above, that one exception is "sexual immorality." If a spouse commits the "sexual immorality" referred to in Matthew 5:32 and Matthew 19:9 then the innocent spouse is scripturally permitted (though not required) to seek a divorce.

Then that answers our question, doesn't it? Obviously, pornography is sexually immoral; therefore you can divorce your husband over his porn addiction, right?

Not quite.

The English term "sexual immorality" is a much broader phrase than what the Greek word used in scripture implies. In our common usage we read the words "sexual" (associated with sex) and "immorality" (the practice of immoral acts, contrasting to that which is ethical, godly, pure, and decent) and it's easy to conclude that pornography is an immoral act related to sex, therefore it fits the "sexual immorality" Jesus spoke of as a cause for divorce.

Is that, in fact, what this passage means? In my opinion, this is a case where translations can cause more confusion than clarity to the reader. Let's look at the wording Jesus actually used.

The word translated in the NKJV and ESV as "sexual immorality" is translated as "unchastity" in the NASB, and "fornication" in the KJV and ASV. The original Greek word used is "porneia."

God was very intentional in the words He chose for both the Old and New Testaments. When He uses a word, the specific meaning of that word is significant. We can only know exactly what God expects of us by studying the exact words He chose and how they fit with the rest of scripture. To figure out what Jesus meant in Matthew 5:32 we should go back and study exactly what Jesus said.

What does this Greek word "porneia" mean in these passages regarding divorce? Thayer defines this word as:

1) illicit sexual intercourse
1a) adultery, fornication, homosexuality, lesbianism, intercourse with animals etc.
1b) sexual intercourse with close relatives; Lev. 18
1c) sexual intercourse with a divorced man or woman; Mar 10:11, Mar 10:12

Thayer and Strong's further point out that "porneia" is from "porneo" which Thayer's defines as:

1) to prostitute one's body to the lust of another
2) to give one's self to unlawful sexual intercourse
2a) to commit fornication
3) metaphorically to be given to idolatry, to worship idols
3a) to permit one's self to be drawn away by another into idolatry

The Greek word Jesus used is very specific. "Porneia" means illicit, physical intercourse with someone outside the bounds of marriage. Christ was explicit when He was speaking to these Pharisees: Unless someone is divorcing for the cause of their spouse having sexual intercourse with someone not in their marriage, then that divorce is outside of God's allowance.

When we look at the definition for the one reason Christ said it was acceptable to seek divorce and compare it to the definition for pornography they simply don't match. Fornication is "illicit sexual intercourse." Pornography is "The presentation of sexual behavior in books, pictures, films, or other media solely to cause sexual excitement." Fornication is not pornography and pornography is not fornication.

Is pornography "sexual immorality" as we use the expression today? Yes, it is a sexually related, immoral activity, the opposite of that which is pure and godly. Is it "porneia" – physical intercourse? No, it is not. Therefore, despite the poor translations which render the specific word "porneia" as the unspecific term "sexual immorality," pornography addiction does not fall under the exception Jesus gave for divorce in Matthew 5:32 and Matthew 19:9.

All sexually related sins are "sexual immorality" but not all sexual immorality is fornication. Lust, pornography, self-gratification, dressing in seductive clothes, sexting, phone sex, touching and viewing things to which you have no right is all sexual immorality, but these are not the sexual intercourse of the Greek word for "fornication."

Strong's says of the word translated in the KJV as "fornication": "harlotry (including adultery and incest); figuratively idolatry." Thayer's calls it "illicit sexual intercourse." This is far from the definition of pornography, in which media is used "solely to cause sexual excitement."

Fornication (porneia) and pornography are not the

same thing. They are both sins that are sexual in nature, but they are not the same sexual sin. Jesus did not say, "Whosoever shall put away his wife, saving for the cause of any sin of a sexual nature," although that is what some have concluded based on poor translations of these scriptures. The Greek word used is very specific. Divorcing one's husband for any cause other than his act of physical intercourse outside of marriage is contrary to Matthew 5:31-32.

Some go so far as to say you can divorce for any reason, misconstruing 1 Corinthians 7:11 as the basis for their argument. "But even if she does depart, let her remain unmarried or be reconciled to her husband." The argument is that this verse gives license to divorce for any cause as long as she doesn't remarry. However, the sentences just before and after this phrase show that is not the case. The last portion of verse 10 states "A wife is not to depart from her husband." And the end of verse 11 commands "a husband is not to divorce his wife." Paul, inspired by the Spirit, clearly states that the divorce should not take place.

We know the Bible never contradicts itself. This passage is in perfect harmony with Matthew 19:9, which specifically says divorce is permitted only in cases of fornication.

> *And I say unto you, Whosoever shall put*
> *away his wife, **except it be for fornication**,*
> *and shall marry another, committeth adul-*
> *tery: and whoso marrieth her which is put*

away doth commit adultery (emphasis
mine).

To say that 1 Corinthians 7:11 broadens the allowance for divorce would mean that those two passages are contradictory and that Jesus failed to mention you could divorce for "fornication OR [fill in the blank]." But Jesus didn't say "fornication or…" He said "except it be for fornication." Therefore we must understand 1 Corinthians 7 in light of that limitation.

1 Corinthians 7:11 takes into consideration the fact that there are times when people divorce for unscriptural reasons. "A wife is not to depart from her husband. But if she does depart…" Paul here gives instruction on how to proceed in these situations. A woman who has wrongly divorced her husband has not committed an unforgivable sin, however she must either reconcile with her husband or live with the consequence of remaining forever single.

Interpretations Must be Consistent

"But wait, wait, wait!" some will contend. "Didn't Jesus say in Matthew 5:27-28 that lust is the same as adultery? So, doesn't that mean lusting after porn is a scriptural reason for divorce?"

Again, let's go directly to the scriptures.

You have heard that it was said to those of
old, "You shall not commit adultery." But I
say to you that whoever looks at a woman
to lust for her has already committed adul-

tery with her in his heart
(Matthew 5:27-28).

Jesus makes it plain in this passage that lust is adultery of the heart. The unfaithfulness is not physical as in fornication, but a condition of the heart. Christ's point here is that lust is just as sinful as the physical act of adultery. While the legalistic Pharisees would claim righteousness for having refrained from sex outside of marriage, Jesus calls out their impurity by condemning their lustful thoughts as being just as evil.

While Jesus did say lust is adultery of the heart, He did not say the earthly consequence of adultery of the heart is the same as that of physical adultery. Lust is sin that separates one from God. Pornography is a sin that damns one's soul to Hell unless there is repentance. But it is not the cause of divorce Christ gives in Matthew 19:9; 5:32; Mark 10:11-12; or Luke 16:18.

If the consequences for adultery of the heart are the same as the consequences for physical adultery, then one must read the verses above this passage with equal consistency. Read what Jesus says of anger in Matthew 5:21-22:

You have heard that it was said to those of
old, "You shall not murder, and whoever
murders will be in danger of the judg-
ment." But I say to you that whoever is an-
gry with his brother without cause shall be
in danger of the judgment. And whoever
says to his brother, "Raca!" shall be in

danger of the council. But whoever says,
"You fool!" shall be in danger of hell fire
(Matthew 5:21-22).

Jesus here compares unjust anger to murder, just as He compares lust to adultery a few verses down. The logic applied to these two passages must be consistent. If the earthly consequence of adultery of the heart is the same as for physical adultery (a spouse's right to divorce), then the earthly consequence of anger without cause must logically be the same as the consequence for murder.

In 1 John 3:15 we find that God equates hatred with murder. "Whoever hates his brother is a murderer, and you know that no murderer has eternal life abiding in him." Interestingly, I've never heard anyone use Matthew 5:21-22 or 1 John 3:15 as grounds for capital punishment for those who hate their brothers. Why? Because we understand Jesus is making a spiritual application here. Spiritually, unjust anger is just as wrong and sinful as murder. Spiritually, lust is just as wrong and sinful as adultery. Both lead to spiritual death and separation from the Father. But the physical, earthly results of these sins are not equal. Anger does not result in execution. Neither does lust result in a right to divorce.

James 4:4 also uses adultery to drive home a point.

Adulterers and adulteresses! Do you not
know that friendship with the world is en-
mity with God? Whoever therefore wants to

be a friend of the world makes himself an
enemy of God.

James compares friendship with the world to adultery, calling those who love the world adulterers and adulteresses. Do you then have a right to divorce your husband on the grounds that he is a "friend of the world"? Clearly not. Similarly, though Christ compares lust with adultery, this does not give His blessing for divorce over pornography. Friendship with the world is not literally the same as adultery. Neither is lust literally the same exact thing as adultery.

The point of these verses is the equal severity of committing these sins. Jesus is not saying that if you hate your brother you have committed physical murder, or that if you lust you have committed physical adultery. The eternal consequences of hatred and murder are the same. The two are equally deserving of eternal damnation. In the same way, the eternal consequences of lust and adultery are the same. In view of eternity, lust equals adultery, but lust does not give a right to divorce any more than hatred receives the sentence of execution.

In Matthew 5:27-28, Jesus is talking about having a heart of obedience to God. He tells the Pharisees they can't go about looking at women other than their wives and act like God does not mind or have a law against it. Just like your husband can't go looking at other women, online or in person, and act like it's "just something guys do." It is sin. It is lust. It is adultery of the heart. It separates his soul from God. It drives a wedge in your relationship, separating the two of you from the union God designed for your marriage. But it does not allow you to give up on your marriage and file for divorce. Claiming Matthew 5:27-28 gives me a right to divorce my husband for a porn addiction is rewriting scripture to fit my circumstances, rather than looking to God's Word for truth.

If Your Husband Leaves

Not all divorce is sinful. God Himself divorced Israel when Israel committed spiritual harlotry. I think it's important to mention, however, that God did not divorce His people until Israel had committed the actual act of worshipping false gods.

> *And I said, after she had done all these things, "Return to Me." But she did not return. And her treacherous sister Judah saw it. Then I saw that for all the causes for which backsliding Israel had committed adultery, I had put her away and given her a certificate of divorce; yet her treacherous sister Judah did not fear, but went and played the harlot also. So it came to pass through her casual harlotry, that she defiled the land and committed adultery with stones and trees. And yet for all this her treacherous sister Judah has not turned to me with her whole heart, but in pretense, says the Lord (Jeremiah 3:7-10).*

Israel spiritually "cheated on" God worshipping other gods. God did not divorce them for being tempted to stray from Him, nor did He divorce them for lusting after all the things they perceived these false gods could provide. It wasn't until they committed the actual act of spiritual infidelity that God put them away through a divorce from the covenant relationship He had made with them. Even then, God (as the injured party) was longsuffering with them and worked to bring about reconciliation despite hundreds of years of infidelity. If we are to follow God's example, divorce ought to be a last resort, sought only after attempts to reconcile with an unfaithful spouse have failed.

If your spouse has not committed physical, sexual intercourse outside of your marriage, you do not have biblical grounds for divorce. However, in some cases, it is not the innocent wife who initiates the divorce but the guilty husband. Porn often escalates until the user is left disconnected, depressed, or simply fed up with life. Sometimes a man will seek to medicate his pain and pursue his selfish desires by leaving his wife, even if he has not committed adultery.

What's a wife to do in such a situation?

First, take heart from the encouragement found in 1 Peter 3:1-2.

> *Wives, likewise, be submissive to your hus-*
> *bands, that even if some do not obey the*
> *word, they, without a word, may be won by*
> *the conduct of their wives, when they ob-*

> *serve your chaste conduct accompanied by fear.*

If your husband has decided to leave you, you still have the opportunity to win him back by your obedience to the Lord and example of purity. A wife who walks honorably before God is powerful. She can draw a wayward husband back to Christ. Your determination to act righteously has the potential to change your husband's mind about leaving. Don't underestimate how the providence of God can work as your husband observes your chaste, submissive behavior. If your husband currently shows no desire to remain in your marriage be patient and pray. Perhaps he will be won by your faithful life before God.

Of course, if your husband carries through with the divorce, there is nothing you can do to stop him. That is not sin on your part. He has chosen to break his vows and go the way of the world. While this would not give you the right to remarry, it does not make you guilty of an unscriptural divorce. You cannot force your husband to remain in your marriage (1 Corinthians 7:15), therefore the guilt of sin would be on your husband, not you.

This is a case where lustful desire has been allowed to grow until it brings about the death of your marriage, and ultimately (if he remains unrepentant) death to your husband's soul.

> *Then, when desire has conceived, it gives birth to sin; and sin, when it is full-grown, brings forth death (James 1:15).*

If your husband leaves, the only thing you can do is remain faithful to God, pray for your husband's soul, and be willing to reconcile should your husband come to repentance.

If you are one who finds herself facing abandonment, the road before you is long and rough. Cling to the Savior! He will carry you.

> *Cast your burden on the Lord, and He shall*
> *sustain you; He shall never permit the*
> *righteous to be moved (Psalm 55:22).*

What If It's More Than Porn?

> *Marriage is honorable among all, and the*
> *bed undefiled; but fornicators and adulter-*
> *ers God will judge (Hebrews 13:4).*

The final stage of porn addiction is sexually acting out. Viewing material that sexually excites him plants ideas which become obsessions. At first it is only fantasy, and it can stay at this level for years, but unchecked thoughts become actions. What do you do if your husband's sexual addiction has taken him further than just pornography? What if he has committed adultery?

Oh, what a heartbreaking situation to be in! To know that your husband has been with another woman brings damage that I can't pretend to understand. If your husband has committed adultery, you have every biblical right to divorce him. That is within your power, and you are not in sin for making that choice. Still, divorce is a choice which requires careful prayer and consideration. Is he repentant? We are called to forgive those who seek biblical reconciliation. Is the adultery continuous? Does he refuse to be faithful? You may need to end the marriage. However, even when adultery is involved there is hope for healing. Much depends on whether the guilty party is willing to do what it takes to stop the sin and get help for the addiction.

I once knew a couple who, from all outward appearances, were very happy together. Surprisingly, it came out that the husband was having an affair with a neighbor. His wife chose to continue to treat him with the love and respect she knew God wanted her to show. He wanted a divorce. She continued to fight for their marriage. He moved out. She didn't give up. Today, they are a strong couple with a beautiful marriage. Could she have scripturally divorced him? Yes. But he probably never would have repented had she not consistently acted with Christ's love toward him. In their case, the reward for her commitment to loving him as Christ would is a happy marriage that is a Heavenly example to their children.

This is not always the case. You cannot force someone to remain married to you any more than you can force him to be faithful. Sometimes letting go is necessary. In any case, the decision to divorce requires careful thought and objective study. It will affect many generations to come.

The Right Question
When people begin a conversation on porn addic-

tion in marriage by seeking permission for divorce, they are starting with the wrong question. Instead of asking "Does my husband's pornography use give me cause for divorce?" we really should be asking, "How can we build a God-honoring marriage despite our history of sin?" We need to train our children and ourselves to ask this question throughout marriage, no matter what sin has been committed. "How do we build a godly marriage regardless of the sin that has been brought into our lives?"

This doesn't mean pornography is not serious. It is a deadly threat to marriage. Saying that porn use alone does not give one a right to divorce does not minimize the sinful effects of lust on relationships. However, pornography is no worse of a sin than any other so far as one's eternity is concerned. We all bring sin into our marriages. Regardless of the nature of the sin, the guilty party needs to repent and cease from unrighteousness— and the spouse needs to forgive and be willing to reconcile.

This is bigger than you or your marriage. Your children and others around you are watching your example. They will see the commitment and forgiveness you extend toward your spouse, and it will affect future generations in more ways than you can ever know. A legacy of divorce is devastating. It reaches far beyond the relationships you see now. When one spouse is from a broken home a couple has a 50% higher risk of divorce. When both spouses are from broken homes, the couple has an astounding 200% higher risk of divorce.[36] You do not want that legacy for your children's children. You can help your children avoid heartache by leaving a legacy of forgiveness.

This is a tough topic, and very personal for nearly every family in America. It does require continual study. But let's start the study with the right questions. Let's first seek to rebuild and restore, no matter what sin has taken place. If approached first with a heart of submission, forgiveness, and faith that God can use even the most broken marriage for His glory, most marriages will never need to consider whether they have proper cause for divorce. It will be irrelevant, because they will be too busy putting their efforts into making their marriages a picture of Christ and the church.

Confessions of a Former Porn Addict

Pornography put me in a state of depression and despair. It made me feel like there was no hope for tomorrow, that there was no way I could ever stop, no way my wife could ever forgive, no way to keep from hurting her again, no way that even if she stayed now she would stay next time. There was no way! No way! No way!

---

[36] "Everything You Need to Know About Divorce – Facts, Statistics, and Rates." Wilkinson & Finkbeiner Family Law Attorneys. No. 72. www.wf-lawyers.com/divorce-statistics-and-facts (accessed September 25, 2018).

My addiction left two people completely devoid of hope, the user and the betrayed. Sin made it so easy to believe that tomorrow held nothing but misery. I had to understand just what this mindset was: Satan's tools of destruction. Not reality.

Before I told Brittany, I *knew* I couldn't quit. I might temporarily pause looking at, reading, and seeking pornography, but I wasn't going to just stop it and never go back. I *knew* I would always go back again, and again, and again. But I still desired to stop hurting Brittany. This led to all sorts of dark "solutions." Maybe I could just up and leave without a word and go start another life, send her money now and again without her knowing where I was. Or I could force Brittany into divorcing me by having her catch me with another woman in our bed. Surely then she would have to leave me—and at least I wouldn't drag her down, too.

I was desperate, and desperate people do not think clearly. I needed to do something to stop hurting Brittany, but quitting pornography didn't seem like an option. Thankfully, by God's grace I never acted on any of my extreme solutions and I did that which was most reasonable, righteous, and truly the only course to take. I told Brittany and I stopped using pornography. I turned to God with all my brokenness and begged Him to forgive me and keep me from destroying those I loved most dearly. I truly cannot imagine what our lives would look like if I had acted on any of my insane and destructive ideas. I am eternally thankful that Brittany chose to stick with me. Our marriage now is better than it ever was before.

CHAPTER 12:
THE BROKEN ROAD

It was all too familiar. I was primping myself for our long-anticipated date. We hardly ever get away by ourselves, and I was thrilled for the opportunity to go out to dinner, just my husband and me. I hurriedly styled my hair and picked out an outfit I hoped would still fit after the birth of our fifth child. The baby wailed, my mascara was half applied, and the dog loudly announced Joshua's arrival home from work.

Skipping the eye liner, I stepped out into the hall to greet Joshua with a smile. His dark eyes met mine and my heart stopped. The children tugged at him and chattered a mile a minute, but he didn't hear a word. "Hold on, kids. Go get yourselves a snack. I need to talk to Mama alone."

I almost prayed that someone had died.

Joshua motioned me into his study. I picked up the screaming baby and followed, sure I knew what was coming. He shut the door and began. "I don't know how it happened."

I was already livid, "How WHAT happened?"

"I don't know. It happened so fast. Some guy at work told me a sex joke and then–"

"But what did YOU do?" I had no patience for the details. I didn't care about what had proceeded whatever had happened. I just wanted to know what had happened. "Just tell me what you did, Joshua!"

"That's what I'm trying to do!"

I didn't need to hear the rest. I had a pretty good idea of what he was going to say, and he wasn't saying it fast enough. "Why?" I begged to know, "Why tonight?"

"Just let me tell you what happened!"

My heart pounded. I felt sick all over, just like that afternoon four years before when he came home from work to tell me his porn addiction wasn't over. We had done this before. I was heartbroken before he began. *This will never be over.*

Is Relapse Inevitable?

Porn addiction is like any other addiction. There are likely to be relapses. Few people successfully quit porn cold turkey with never a backward glance. That doesn't mean it is inevitable that your husband will repeatedly stumble back into porn. When God says to keep oneself pure, He expects complete purity. He knows it will be difficult, but if He said your husband can break free from sin, then he can break completely free without returning. Your husband is not *destined* to return to porn. Unfortunately, the reality is that relapse is not rare. It is more common than not. Your husband is only human. He fumbles and fails, just like you.

The nation of Israel in the Old Testament is a classic example of the cycle of sin. The book of Judges chronicles the sequence of Israel's unfaithfulness, return to God, and eventual return to sin. Israel started out serving God faithfully, but before too long they fell into idolatry and other sins. The consequence was bondage to foreign nations. Israel would then cry out to the Lord, and He would provide judges for deliverance. The Israelites then returned to serving the Lord. But before too long... The cycle continued time after time.

It is the same with us. We serve the Lord. We fall into sin. The consequences of our own sin drive us to seek deliverance from the Father. He forgives us, and we return to serving Him only to give into temptation again.

An addiction to pornography often follows this same cycle. Strong resolve is weakened by years of habitual surrender. When finally the "pain exceeds the pleasure" it drives a God-fearing man to his knees. He seeks a way out through repentance. God grants the mercy of forgiveness and he is restored to a right fellowship with the Father. When he has turned, he is strengthened. But the memory of habitual surrender is still there to remind him that pleasure is only a glance away.

Enormous guilt is placed on women by themselves, by society, and to an extent by the church for continued porn addictions. Doubts and accusations of, "If you had only done this," or, "If you hadn't done that," assail from every corner, most incessantly from your own mind. Silence those voices.

It is not your fault.

You are not to blame.

You are not your husband's sin.

A flawless recovery is an idealistic hope, not the determining factor of the viability of your marriage. The important thing is that your husband remains open with you and willing to repent if he does fall back into sin. The difference in your husband after his initial repentance of his pornography use should be marked. Where defensiveness once was, humility should now be obvious. If he has stumbled but is truly repentant he will honestly confess where he has failed and recommit to keeping his eyes on Christ. As long as he remains willing to repent and seeks greater measures of protection and accountability, there is hope for ultimate recovery.

Suspicions, Suspicions

My husband has struggled in the past. I have no specific evidence that he has started looking at pornography again, but I have my suspicions. What do I do?

There are usually warning signs when a man has fallen back into porn use, or was never serious about getting out to begin with. If your husband exhibits symptoms of continued addiction, you are right to be concerned. Some of those red flags are:

- Refusing to install filters and accountability software
- Lying about small things
- Resistance to the idea of an accountability part-

ner

- Excusing poor entertainment choices
- Showing signs of depression such as oversleeping or isolation
- Severe mood swings

If you suspect your husband has been looking at porn, the first thing to do is simply ask him. That is sometimes enough for a man to come clean when he otherwise lacked the courage. Or, he may have reasonable explanations to ease your doubts.

Doubt is often simply a response to fear. If you are afraid your husband will stumble, you may overreact to innocent situations. If your husband has not exhibited the symptoms above but you still feel nagging doubt, approach your husband with your fears. He may admit he has stumbled, or he may deny that he has done anything sinful, at which point you have to make a decision about whether or not to trust him.

Trust, to a great extent, is a decision we make. You can never know with full certainty if your husband is staying one hundred percent clean. You cannot read his heart. You have to decide whether his words, actions, and attitudes lean more toward honesty or deceit. You have to come to a conclusion about whether you can believe your husband is telling the truth based on what you know of his character.

You know your husband better than anyone. Gauge his response. Do you have trouble believing him? Try to determine whether that is merely because of his history, or whether something concrete is making you uneasy. It may just be that you are going through a period where trust is difficult for you. Even couples who consider their marriage to have recovered from betrayal trauma sometimes go through phases where the wife is concerned about her husband's faithfulness. Don't be surprised if you have moments of suspicion even years down the road. Certain times of year or particular circumstances might trigger suspicion even when it is unwarranted.

To finish the story of our date night, I was finally quiet long enough to allow Joshua to tell me what had happened. What had he done? Nothing. Absolutely nothing. He hadn't come home to tell me he had looked at porn. He hadn't intended to make me think that at all. He had come to talk to me because a guy at work had offhandedly told a sexually explicit joke. It made Joshua uncomfortable and fearful that he might be tempted to look at porn. He said it felt too familiar, reminded him too much of the days when he enjoyed crass innuendoes. He wanted to be sure he told me before he allowed the story to lead him into lust.

My overreaction was triggered by the fact that he came home very similarly to how he came home the day he told me he had been using pornography. That particular "we need to talk" approach triggered fear and panic and hurled me into reliving the moment he revealed his addiction.

That painful experience led me to acknowledge

two truths. First, it gave me more confidence than ever that Joshua's porn addiction is under control. I have greater trust now that he will tell me when he struggles. Second, I was right – this will never be over. I wanted to be done with pornography. I didn't want to ever think about it again. I wanted to act like it never existed. But it's a permanent fact of our history together, and it continues to impact our relationship. In that way, it's never really over.

You may always have moments of doubt and fear, but they will become fewer and further between as your husband continues to prove his faithfulness. You may continue to experience triggers that remind you of the pain you've been through but, as trust grows, pornography will not be a constant cloud over your marriage.

Remember that forgiveness does not equal trust. Forgiving your husband for looking at porn does not mean you will immediately trust him. Trust can be slowly restored as your husband continues to show his faithfulness. If you suspect your husband is looking at pornography again, ask him. Check up on him. Determine whether anything specific is making you doubt his fidelity. If you can't put a finger on it, do your best to trust his word. Keep your eyes open. You won't have any trouble being alert for a little while. But if there is nothing there, try to relax. Choose to trust until your trust is proven misplaced.

Confronting Your Husband

In 2013, my husband came to me and confessed

everything of his own accord. Things had seemed a bit off, but I had not actually found any pornographic material on our devices. Joshua was the one to reveal his continued addiction. Because of that, I felt a sense of security that even if he did begin looking at porn again, he would eventually come clean and tell me.

If your husband has come to you and admitted his struggle with pornography, count yourself blessed. There is so much hope in that situation. It means he wants out of it. Trust is so much easier to rebuild when you know that the shame of his own sin drove him out of secrecy. His conscience has not yet been completely seared. Hold onto the comfort that he has a tender heart and he truly desires to be free.

Not every woman has this comfort. Even if he was the one to initiate the original confession, he might not be as brave in the future. The majority of wives find out about their husband's porn addictions because they either catch them in the act or they unsuspectingly stumble across his search history. It is often the same story when finding out about repeated use after his confession. What do you do if you (or someone else) discover your husband's pornographic material?

While there is no comfort in the discovery, it's certainly not hopeless if you are the one who discovers your husband's porn use first. It doesn't necessarily mean he doesn't want to change, or even that he wouldn't have eventually come forward. Many men are waiting to be found out. They want to be discovered.

They want their wives to know but they lack the courage to reveal their continued struggle.

As the details of Joshua's involvement in pornography came out, he told me he had often left images open on his phone, hoping I would find them and stop him. He felt completely helpless to quit, and he hoped that by me discovering the images for myself, he could finally come clean and break free. For over a year he didn't have the courage to come forward himself, but he prayed – yes, actually prayed – that I would discover his sin.

If a man returns to his addiction after already confessing and repenting of porn use he may be so ashamed that he feels he cannot face his wife with another confession. If he lacks the nerve to come to her himself he may choose to become less and less careful about covering up his tracks, hoping somebody – anybody – will catch him and force him to quit. Of course, it's a vain hope. Nobody will force your husband to quit. That's up to him. But many men think that if they continue looking at pornography until their wives catch them then they will finally be able to stop. It's a despairing hope coming from a heart that is aching to quit, but a mind that will not turn away. It's the character of addiction.

If you have found evidence that your husband has been looking at porn you must confront him. Do not simply hope it will go away, or that it was a one-time "mistake." Bring the evidence to him and ask him to give account for his actions.

My friend Sheila experienced this several years ago. Things had seemed a little strange for a few days and finally, putting two and two together, she realized where the evidence was leading. When she did a history search and discovered just how often her husband, Mike, had been looking at porn on their personal computer over the last few weeks, she was devastated. This wasn't the first time she had made such a discovery. Every time she confronted Mike he promised it would be the last. This time she had to demand a change.

Sheila sent the kids to a neighbor's house to play and waited for Mike to get home from work. When he arrived, Sheila wasted no time in demanding an account of his pornography use. Mike had no choice but to admit that an unintentional glance at a sidebar ad had spiraled into a return to his addiction. He was relieved Sheila had discovered his sin. This time Sheila demanded Mike get counseling and an accountability partner, as well as filtering software on all devices. Several years later, Mike has remained clean.

If you have evidence that your husband is using pornography again, you must prepare your heart and mind for a confrontation. Nothing is gained by pretending like it is not happening or hoping he will eventually quit on his own. Addiction always escalates. The sooner you confront your husband, the greater his chances of getting help to quit.

Prepare for the confrontation. Before you approach your husband, pray. Pray, pray, pray! Pray for wisdom, control over your words, a humble heart, readiness to forgive, the right opportunity to speak, and strength to hear the truth. Pray for your husband to be humbled, to honestly confess all, and to be willing to take steps to break his addiction.

Pray over how you will proceed. Have a plan for what you will do during and after the confrontation. This will help you keep a tighter rein on your emotions and handle the situation as objectively as possible. How you proceed will, of course, partly depend on his response to the confrontation, but it is wise to have an idea of what you will do next. Will you take it to the church? Inform his family of the addiction? Insist he enroll in a rehab program? Take some time to consider your plan of action beforehand.

Fortify your soul with scripture and prayer before you confront your husband. Be sure your heart is right before God, and do your best to remain as calm as possible. Eat something. Rest. Breathe. A well-nourished, rested mind will be much more capable of calm discussion.

Seek a time when you can be away from your children. My friend Sheila was wise to send their children to a friend's house. If you have children, they do not need to overhear the details of their daddy's porn use. Emotions will be high, and the atmosphere will be tense. Even very young children can pick up on that. Getting them out of the house will protect their emotions as well as allow you the space you need to focus on the conversation without distraction. Prevent interruptions by choosing a time to approach your husband when the children are not around to detract from the discussion.

If you feel the need, take someone with you. It is difficult to confront another person's sin, and perhaps even more difficult to be confronted. If your husband is unresponsive, in denial, or angry at your questions, seek another person to mediate between you. This is serious business, and it can also be volatile. If you feel the need for a witness or emotional support, contact an elder or trusted friend who is willing to sit with you while you approach your husband.

If he is unrepentant, take it to the church. Matthew 18:15-17 outlines the steps for confronting someone in unrepentant sin.

> *Moreover if your brother sins against you, go and tell him his fault between you and him alone. If he hears you, you have gained your brother. But if he will not hear, take with you one or two more, that 'by the mouth of two or three witnesses every word may be established.' And if he refuses to hear them, tell it to the church. But if he refuses even to hear the church, let him be to you like a heathen and a tax collector.*

If your husband is a Christian who refuses to acknowledge or repent of the sin of pornography, these steps apply. After the initial confrontation, take two or three witnesses with you. If he still refuses to listen and repent, tell his sin to the church. If he continues to be unrepentant, the church then has a responsibility to dis-fellowship your husband.

Thankfully, most Christian men do not take it that far. This is not a guarantee that he will not stumble in the future, but as long as he remains repentant there can be forgiveness and hope that he will one day be completely free from pornography.

When It Never Seems to End

What if he doesn't quit? What if you catch him with pornography again. And again. And again? As we studied in the last chapter, unless there has been physical adultery you do not have the right to divorce. So, what do you do when it seems your husband will never give up his addiction to pornography?

I received a message this week from Michelle. She wrote to me with inspiring courage, and gave me permission to share her story. What follows is an account of hope in the face of repeated heartbreak.

Michelle's Story

My husband and I weren't Christians when we met and married. It wasn't a secret that he watched pornography when we married, and I didn't think it was that big of a deal. For him it was a gateway into sexual addiction. I discovered several emotional affairs (women who lived far away that he had no chance of being close to). They would exchange "I love you's." He went on a date with another woman when I was pregnant with our son. I thought he was just visiting an old friend, and I didn't think much about it. When I asked him to come home because I was having contractions, he said he would, but he stayed another hour or so to be with her. That was the beginning of serious problems for us.

He had an inappropriate friendship with the woman who introduced us. She would visit him at work, and he wouldn't tell me. He'd go out for drinks with her and tell me he was going alone. He'd stay home from work all day without telling me, and he was gone all day at least one day on the weekends (I wasn't allowed to call him while he was gone). He refused to be intimate with me. He would, however, watch pornography and be intimate with himself. I felt cheated. It didn't bother me as much as long as I felt wanted and my needs were being met, but when he refused sex with me for over six months, it became a serious problem.

My health deteriorated to the point where I was sick more often than I was well, and I lost my job. It was in this time period that we became Christians. We threw away all the porn, and he stopped drinking. However, he continued to withhold intimacy. He continued to have inappropriate relationships with other women. He also admitted to watching pornography and masturbating in the bathroom at work every day, but I had to literally beg him to be with me.

We followed the right biblical steps. I confronted him personally, then took two witnesses with me. We went through a few marriage counselors at the request of those witnesses. The first was a kook. The second, I felt, actually helped. I felt like things were moving in the right direction. He still wasn't being open and honest in any facet of our relationship. He was still being secretive with our finances, with his text messages, with his Facebook account, etc. I had been given access to his online accounts but not his bank account. We'd taken out a large loan to pay for a trip to the Mayo Clinic for me. Due to the stress from all of this, I was having serious health issues. When his parents offered to help ease the burden of our trip, he blew all of that money on I still don't know what. I think a fair amount was spent meeting his other woman or paying for pornography online.

A Change

He changed jobs without telling me or consulting me right after I lost my job, and he ended up only making about $60 a week total. We had two children to care for, and I was medically unable to work at that point. We ended up moving to another state for work. His financial habits were such that we were seriously in the hole, and I had no idea why. When we moved, he couldn't even get a bank account. I took over our finances, and that made me feel a little more secure. He kept a secret bank account, though, and his mom regularly (and secretly) put hundreds of dollars per month into that account. I have no idea what he spent that money on, but it was at a time when I was struggling to feed our children while trying to pay down my medical debt and all of his secret maxed-out credit cards. We couldn't afford for him to spend money on himself but, at the time, he felt like he was entitled.

I thought a geographic move would get him away from the other woman, but after only six months of living here, I found a message from her. It was clear from her message that he had been complaining to her about what a terrible wife I was. At the time, I could hardly get out of bed. When I wasn't sick, I was too depressed to move, and we couldn't afford my medication for either condition. I'd had to move away from my support group, my family, and my church family because of his poor decisions. I went to my preacher here, desperate for help (we don't currently have elders), and he spoke to my husband. My husband denied that he'd ever been physically unfaithful, and my preacher told me I was stuck with him.

I felt like nothing would ever change. It had been
five years of emotional torture at that point, and
it felt like he didn't even care. His boss found out
what was going on because his performance was
affected. I was ready to separate after finding
him having inappropriate conversations with at
least 13 women, and after five years of him
choosing pornography or just himself over me.
Anyway, his boss forced him to go to Sexaholics
Anonymous (he had to have a paper signed at
least once a week or he'd be fired). I agreed, on
the advice of our preacher to go to marriage
counseling again. I joined S-Anon to meet with
partners of people with addictions like my husband's.

While I ultimately decided that S-Anon was not
for me, I did learn a lot. My husband learned a
lot from being in S-Anon as well. We learned
that his addiction stemmed from an inappropriate
introduction to sexuality (his father handed him a
Playboy at a young age to explain sex), lack of
religious upbringing, and a serious fear of rejec-
tion. They said that the refusal to have physical
or emotional intimacy with me was called "sexual anorexia," and, for him, it was because he was
too afraid to get close to me for fear that I would
reject him.

When our relationship progressed beyond a certain point, he was too scared that I would reject

him sexually or emotionally, so he rejected me instead. He carried on with nameless, faceless women in pornography because they could never reject him since they weren't really there. He engaged with women there was no possible future with because they also couldn't reject him in any meaningful way. He's still terrified to tell me the truth about anything he thinks he could get in "trouble" about with me, from things that are stupid to serious things.

When we went to counseling, I refused to sit in the same room with him. We each took half the hour allotted. I just refused to sit and cry in front of him in the counselor's office ever again. I'd already spent so much time doing that, and I couldn't handle him seeing the pain he'd caused and not caring anymore. That's how it felt. Like I showed him my deepest, darkest pain, and he pretended to care in the counselor's office but refused to enact any meaningful change. It hurt so much more when we'd make an agreement with the counselor and he'd renege as soon as we left because he just didn't feel comfortable doing it (as if I felt totally comfortable doing whatever they'd asked myself.)

A Ray of Hope

It took a long time, but I feel like we finally found a healthy place. I can ask him now if he's watched pornography, and he answers me honestly. I've promised not to get upset if he just tells me the truth. I asked him today just out of curiosity because it's been quite some time since I checked in on him. He said that several months ago he clicked on some kind of click bait with women in their underwear or swimsuit models. That's miles better than the hardcore porn he used to watch, though we both agree that those pictures are as inappropriate as the videos he used to watch.

When I found out he was still doing it after we became Christians, I was angry and felt betrayed. We'd decided together that it was wrong, and we'd gotten rid of all of it that was in the house. I found out he'd been watching it and pleasuring himself while rejecting me for months and months at a time. I thought it must have had something to do with having his baby, because everything had been fine before I'd had our son. I'd been on pelvic rest for the majority of that pregnancy, and I thought maybe the months away had changed things.

There were years that I hated him for what he did. I hated him for letting it go beyond looking and for starting to reach out to real people. I wanted to die. I wanted him to die. I couldn't understand why God gave me this man who seemed like a completely different person after we got married. (Though there were, of course, red flags

I thought about in retrospect that I'd ignored while we were dating.)

I isolated myself from my friends and family, as much because of my illness as because I felt unlovable and so unwanted. I felt like everyone loved him so much more than they loved me, even our children. Friends at church were much more willing to talk to him for hours than to me. Making friends came so easy to him, and it was so hard for me.

I felt like I'd failed at every aspect of my life. I'd failed to be a good wife because I couldn't hold his interest. I'd never been a wife who had ever (not even once) said no to sex in our lives. Had he tried to initiate at any point in our marriage, I never would have turned him down (except during my pregnancy for the safety of our child, but he never attempted to initiate during that time). He had never once attempted to initiate sex. It was always me. I felt like I was the one with a sexual addiction, and he made me feel like I should be going to meetings long before he ever started going.

We had a marriage counselor once who said it was ok to find reasons other than love to stay in our marriage. At the time, I was a stay-at-home mom, and I homeschooled our kids. I had no money to get a place of my own, and having "permission" to stay for financial reasons, even though I couldn't look at him, was somehow liberating.

I really tried to throw myself into religion. I was a new Christian, struggling with a husband I strongly suspected was cheating on me and who was absolutely entangled in sexual sin. I struggled with allowing him to be the head of our household. He was generally unwilling to accept responsibility while accusing me of not being a godly wife because I disrespected him by not allowing him to do his part as the man. I felt like I'd failed God, too. I had no idea what to do because I tried to hand over responsibilities, but my husband would ignore them or refuse to accept them. Then, I'd have to continue to do what I'd been doing and incur his anger because someone had to steer the ship.

Eventually we got to a healthy place where he took control of our family. After a few bumps, he agreed not to make decisions without me (after the job debacle) because God put me in his life for a reason, and he was denying my purpose in his life by not using me as God intended. We made an agreement about sex, too. It's obvious that I'm always going to want it more often than he does, but we agreed that I'd only ask for it when I absolutely had to have it to avoid sexual sin myself. If I ask for it now, he knows it's not just because I love him and want to be close to him but because I actually need it, and we agreed that he cannot refuse. It's somewhere between more than he wants and less than I want, but it works for both of us.

Better Together

I'm actually glad now that I stuck with him. Our marriage is a lot better now than it was in the beginning. The first five years were the worst years of my life. I think, for us, the turning point was when I let him back in after the last contact with the other women (I slept in the other room for eight months and refused to look at him or talk to him for months because I couldn't do it and not say or do something I regretted).

We got pregnant, and I lost our baby. I think he was finally in a place where we were both feeling the same thing, and we had to let each other in to a certain degree. I needed him because I had absolutely no one else. A few months later, we had another surprise pregnancy that ended in heartbreak. I lost my mind with grief. I almost died when we gave birth to that baby, and I think that somehow solidified that I was a human being and that he actually wanted me around to raise our two boys.

We waited several years, strengthened our marriage, and he helped me grieve over our lost babies. While we were trying not to get pregnant earlier this year, God threw us for a loop and blessed us with another baby. We're currently at 25 weeks, and I really do feel like my husband puts me first in his life. I notice that he's usually going somewhere and doing something during his lunch break. He goes to the pet store to play with the animals, or he goes to the guitar store and plays guitars and drums. I think he does things like this to keep his hands busy. He's a lot more open with me, and he's much more devoted to our family. I feel like he's largely become the man I thought I married.

I still have trust issues. We talk pretty openly about it. I still check his emails and Facebook messages periodically. We have rules for conversations with the opposite sex. I always tell him if I talk to a man privately. I had a man who helped me with some Bible study topics who I talked to over Facebook, and I was very open with my husband about it (he gave me permission). Once, my husband said something to me about how he thought I'd leave him for this man I was studying the Bible with, and I cut off those private study conversations. Even though I'd given my husband access to read all of the messages, there's just no reason to make him question me like I used to question him. I know how that feels. I ask that he tells me if he talks to another woman regardless of how innocent the conversation is. We're never alone in the same room as a member of the opposite sex. We never privately phone a member of the opposite sex without reporting to the other that it was done and what was said. Even if it's work related, I ask him to tell me. Even if it's a man contacting me about something church related, I tell him. It's just the right way to handle it.

We do more things together. He doesn't go golfing alone anymore. We go together, even though I don't play. I drive the golf cart and heckle, and he plays. We got interested and invested in each other's activities. I have a non-negotiable 15 minutes of his time every night after the kids go to bed that are just for me. Usually we watch TV together and he lets me lay my head in his lap while he pets my hair. That satisfies my need for physical touch without asking too much from him and doesn't trigger his fear of intimacy. We talk about our feelings a lot. I think he's less scared of talking to me now. I'm less scared of crying in front of him. I feel like he recognizes his selfishness and entitlement early in our marriage and realizes that he was continuing his single life while we were married while I was continuing my life of control in my house from before we were married.

I remember a sermon I heard about difficult marriages. What stuck with me was that the preacher said something about spouses coming to him for counseling and wanting out for whatever reason. He said that the first thing he often said was something along the lines of, "Well, you picked him." I knew that when I said "I do" I chose him, flaws and all. My husband and I can joke now that when we said "for better or for worse" we didn't look at the fine print on the ratio of better to worse. God never promised our marriages would be easy. If our marriage is meant to reflect Christ's relationship with the church, then problems in our marriage often reflect problems in our spiritual walk.

I tried not to blame it all on him, though he was definitely doing something wrong and was going to have to answer to God. The only thing I had control of was my actions and reactions. I wasn't always acting like a godly wife. I nagged, complained, wailed, screamed, and was sometimes pretty awful to him. I tried what Peter wrote about regarding winning your lost husband without a word, even though he became a Christian during his struggle. I tried to remember to forgive him seventy times seven. God's forgiven me more times than I've ever had to forgive my husband. I tried not to look at it based on how much it was hurting me, but rather how much it was hurting God. I remembered that my primary goal as his spouse was to get him to Heaven with me.

I wasn't always perfect. I failed him in that as often as he failed me. My sins were in my reactions to his. Instead of helping a brother who was entangled in sin, I would react negatively and push him further into the arms of the sin that made him feel better temporarily. I had to change my mindset and try to focus on helping him rather than punishing him. That isn't supposed to be my job anyway. I promised to stop getting mad if he told me before I stumbled upon it, and I kept that promise. I prayed for him and I looked for cues that he was struggling.

I think we're both all-in in our marriage now. As for it being worth it, I can say that I couldn't face life without him now. A family member is going through a terrible divorce right now due to adultery, and my heart breaks for them. After I talk to my family member, I look at my husband and say, "Let's never get divorced." It took a long time to get to that point and, honestly, there were times when I would have given anything for a way out. There were times I went totally crazy wanting to plant surveillance everywhere to catch him in the act so I could go live alone or find a husband who'd actually care about me. Ironically, I don't think I'd ever find a man who values me as much as my husband does now, having gone through the fire together. I know he sees where he went wrong and how selfish he was, and he sees how hard I worked to save our marriage. I think he values the love I have for him now that the scales have fallen from his eyes, and I think he works really hard to give back the same love to me.

I know he's going to struggle sometimes. I know he'll likely watch pornography again. He just admitted to looking at inappropriate photos, so I know he still slips. I also see how hard he's trying, and I try to remember that in God's eyes all sin is equal. Whatever sin I'm currently struggling with is just as bad as what he's struggling with. I try to help him with his just like I hope he'll help me with mine. My focus is being the best Christian wife and mother I can be and not on how much it hurts. I know it's ultimately not about me. His porn addiction isn't about our sex life, my body, or our marriage. It's about his feelings of fear, inadequacy, and selfishness. For us, it would have been hard to say at the worst times that it could ever be worth it to stay married. I never would have believed it. I had a friend whose husband had committed adultery, but they had an ideal marriage by the time I knew them. I saw it, but I never would have thought that could be us. Now, I remember all the times I wanted my husband to die so I could be free, and I pray God keeps him around as long as possible because I'll never find someone who treats me better."

Confessions of a Former Porn Addict

It is very odd to me. One day, being a slave to pornography seems so distant, so strange, so foreign to the me of today. Thinking about when I was that way seems more like watching a movie about someone else. But then, the next day, the struggle becomes real again, and I find myself fighting to not fall back into slavery. This makes no sense to me at all. But addiction is that way. A former smoker (30 years clean) told me that the smell of a cigarette makes him gag every time now, yet there are still times when he will finish a meal, and want a cigarette and coffee so badly that he has to resist the temptation to get in his car and go buy a pack. It's so frustrating! You can stop engaging in your addiction, and even learn to despise it—but that doesn't mean you don't still occasionally desire the pleasure that it used to bring. One of the most discouraging parts about trying to quit porn was knowing I would never fully stop wanting it.

I was astounded and encouraged the first time I realized I had gone a couple of days without being tempted by pornography. That was something I didn't think would ever be possible. Now when I do think about it, I find it an annoyance and usually have no trouble pushing it aside. Not always, but usually. I've dreamed about reaching a point when there is simply never any temptation anymore, but I know that won't really come until the next life.

Even when I'm not facing temptation, I know I have to stay on guard. Any situation I get into, I have to look at from the perspective of a former addict. I have to consider how I could be tempted, and make sure I put up road blocks and safety nets. I've devised all sorts of rules for myself and am always on guard to make sure I have a good defensive system in place against Satan. I know the slope into sin begins with things that aren't necessarily sin. It starts with careless thoughts, words, and actions.

One thing I know: It takes work to stay out of sin. Philippians 3:14

> *I press toward the goal for the prize of the upward call of God in Christ Jesus.*

Thayer's Greek definition of 'press' is: "to earnestly endeavor to acquire." Refusing sin is not easy; it takes earnest determination, but it is necessary to get to Heaven. I've read that sin means "missing the mark." I had no problem with that – missing the mark takes no effort. But hitting the mark – that takes skill, desire, and effort.

> *Be sober, be vigilant; because your adversary the Devil walks about like a roaring lion, seeking whom he may devour (1 Peter 5:8).*

I want to hit the mark. I've got to gain the skills and put forth the effort it's going to take. Even though I've been clean for years, I've still got to be intentional about staying away from pornography. Some days are easier than others, but I'm committed to hitting the mark of purity no matter how difficult it gets.

CHAPTER 13:
THE OTHER SIDE OF THE STORM

Hurricane Florence is raging over the Carolinas as I write. Thousands evacuated the east coast this week in preparation for what was predicted to be a Category 4 storm. The torrential rainfall and surging winds have caused a state of emergency as this particularly slow-moving storm creeps along the coast. Flash flooding has already destroyed homes and businesses in a matter of moments. The full extent of the damage is not yet known, nor will it be known for days, but it's already obvious it will take some areas months to recover.

The calm that descends following a spring storm is absent in the wake of a natural disaster such as Florence. Though birds still fly, the sound of their chorus is lost beneath the grind of axes and saws as clean-up crews attempt to restore order to the community. The grass does not sparkle but instead turns to swampy mire as floodwaters slowly recede. Thanks to the relentless downpour, there are no breathtaking scenes of a town refreshed by rain, only a view of destruction.

Where is the beauty in such a catastrophic event?

A different sort of beauty follows natural disasters, one which requires more from us but which renders greater blessings. Amidst the loss and chaos of tragedy, a spirit of unity rises in our communities. Neighbors rally around neighbors. Strangers go out of their way to provide assistance where needed. All ages and all races join hands to rebuild. We do this because we are unified by our experience of pain, and determined to overcome. The beauty after disaster is not found in glowing skies or the scent of fresh air but in the hearts of those committed to helping each other restore what was lost.

The crisis of betrayal is much like a hurricane; powerful, unyielding, and furious. When the worst of the storm is over, what is left? Surveying the damage, you may see nothing but ruin – broken trust, lost dreams, and the debris of failed commitment. There may be moments where it seems like this is the end, there is nothing left.

Don't chase those lies.

The beauty of tragedy is that God can always rebuild. As long as you remain anchored to the Savior, you and your husband can beat this storm. If you turn your hearts to each other and together turn toward God, not even the worst tempest of the soul can destroy your marriage.

You have a long, arduous road ahead. Rebuilding what your husband's pornography addiction tore down will take time. Just as you think you are healing, Satan will shatter your security with temptations, doubts, and fears. You may wonder time and time again why you are fighting for such a difficult, pain-filled marriage. This is why: Because you love God. Because God loves you. Because He has wonderful blessings waiting for you as you walk faithfully with Him.

*I have come that they may have life, and
that they may have it more abundantly
(John 10:10b).*

You will want to quit. Don't. Your marriage is worth fighting for. Don't let Satan steal the blessings God has in store for you. Remember that from the most destructive storm this world has ever known, God gave man a beautiful new beginning and placed His rainbow of promise in the sky. He can give your marriage that same fresh start because, "He who is in you is greater than he who is in the world" (1 John 4:4).

You now know each other's darkest flaws. In fact, by the light of this revelation you probably see them more clearly than anything else. Betrayal amplifies every other problem in marriage. Even what you once considered minor irritations can seem like irreconcilable differences. But if you hold onto God and your spouse, God can make your marriage a glorious example of Christ and the church. When you love each other with agape love, forgiving as you have been forgiven, you are a living picture of the sacrificial love God has for His people.

I remember talking to a friend not long after Joshua's confession. I said, "I just don't know if I married the right guy." Her response made me smile. "Well, whether he's the one you should have married or not, you're married to him now. That ship has sailed, girl. He's your 'right guy' now." She reminded me I had to make the unpopular choice to love my husband regardless of how badly he had hurt me. Her words reminded me of a quote from Kid President. "Two roads diverged in the woods, and I took the road less traveled... and it hurt, man!"

You stand at a juncture with two roads stretched out before you. You can take the path the world often travels, chasing false freedom and empty hopes, running from anything that causes pain. Or, you can take the road Jesus took, the one He asks you to take. That road is gonna hurt, sister, but it's the only one that leads to true peace and healing. Take the road less traveled by, and love your husband on the journey.

Cling to the Lord, dear sister. This is a journey you never chose to take, but He is holding your hand. While you won't wake up tomorrow in a magical world where your husband never hurts you, you can wake up tomorrow knowing that in Christ there is hope for healing. You must lean on the Father now more than ever. He will give you the endurance you need to continue to love your husband unconditionally. Be in the Word daily. Be constantly on your knees. Seek those who will rally around you and hold you up before the throne in prayer. Fully trust in the One who will never break His vows to you. He can make all things new, and He will use your story to His glory.

One day you can be grateful for the pain you are now enduring. Eventually the rain will stop beating and the raging wind will die down. You can then look back at this refining fire and see the splendor of what God creates from the ashes. Hold on. The beauty may not be immediately obvious, but it is there even in the worst situation. It is in your faith, courage, endurance, forgiveness, and commitment to your husband. It is in the rich mercy of our Savior. And it is in the hope Christ has given us that sin can be beaten.

In time you will notice the sun is shining again. The birds are chirping their chorus of praise once more. The grass is even greener now.

Don't you love the beauty that follows a storm?

A Note From the Authors

A crisis in marriage often stirs in our hearts a longing to be close to God. The Lover of our souls longs to be close to you, too. He is the only One who can bring about complete healing in your life. As important as it is to pursue a good relationship with your husband, it is even more important to first seek a relationship with our Holy Father through His plan of salvation. God doesn't just want you to have a happy marriage. He wants you to have eternal life with Him.

God sent Jesus, His own Son, to redeem us (John 3:16). Salvation is found in Christ alone, who gave Himself to die for our sins (Acts 4:12). Faith in Him (which comes through hearing the Gospel – Romans 10:17), leads us to repent of our sins (Acts 3:19), confess Christ as Lord (Romans 10:9), and receive His gift of salvation by having our sins washed away through baptism (Acts 2:38, 22:16; 1 Peter 3:21). Christ gladly offers eternal life to those who submit to His will and live faithfully until death (Revelation 2:10).

If you'd like to learn more about God's plan for your salvation, contact us at: servingfromhome@gmail.com or visit a Church of Christ near you!

ABOUT THE AUTHORS

Joshua and Brittany Richardson live in Wisconsin where Joshua preaches for the St. Croix Valley Church of Christ. Brittany is a stay-at-home mom and home-schools their six children. Josh and Britt blog together at www.thebeatenroad.com, where they provide resources for helping couples recover from porn addiction. They would love to hear from you! You can contact them at servingfromhome@gmail.com.

www.ingramcontent.com/pod-product-compliance
Lightning Source LLC
LaVergne TN
LVHW011321080426
835513LV00006B/147